Real Stories. Real South.

"I have the nerve to walk my own way, however hard, in my search for reality, rather than climb upon the rattling wagon of wishful illusions."

~

Zora Neale Hurston,
in a letter to Countee Cullen, 1943

THE BITTER SOUTHERNER READER, VOL. 2

Published by The Bitter Southerner, Inc.
Atlanta, Georgia

Cover Photo: Greg Dupree

ISBN: 978-0-9980293-0-6

THE BITTER SOUTHERNER READER

VOL. 2

Contents

Conviviality
Aplenty

•••

FOREWORD BY CHUCK REECE

Neither age nor dementia will ever have the strength to make me forget the evening of Thursday, February 12, 2015.

The Bitter Southerner had been around for 18 months, and the University of North Carolina's Center for the Study of the American South had invited me to speak to its students. The night before, friends in Chapel Hill roped me into telling a story at an event called "Bless Your Heart," a spoken-word show for the North Carolina Comedy Arts Festival. After the stories, most of the storytellers retired to a bar on Franklin Street called the Crunkleton. There was conviviality aplenty. Somehow, I even ended up behind the bar with Gary Crunkleton teaching me how to make a classic cocktail called the Blue Blazer. This involves pouring four ounces of flaming Scotch whiskey from one pewter mug to another, repeatedly. Fire!

As the night was ending, I fell into conversation with one storyteller — a man I had not expected to run into so casually, but one of my favorite contemporary Southern writers — Daniel Wallace, the author of "Big Fish" and many other inventive and charming novels. He asked me, "Would you be interested in reading a story I wrote about the time I killed a chicken?"

Chance meetings such as that one have long played a critical role in The Bitter Southerner's ability to expand its cadre of contributing writers. Had you asked me two years earlier if we could get the likes of Wallace into our pages, I would have declared you nuts. But here, in this volume, is "Killings," in which Wallace recounts sending a hen to the great beyond.

This volume of The Bitter Southerner Reader collects our favorite stories from our second full year of existence: 2015.

The topics it covers include: the Southern drawl, why New Orleanians came home after Hurricane Katrina, the deep cultural history of Nashville hot chicken, the life of a Mississippi River guide, reconciliation that comes 40 years after desegregation, trains, grits, the meaning and hope that lies embedded in the granite of Georgia's Stone Mountain, the ghosts of a long-gone ballpark, a farmer with a vision, an oysterman left behind by time and circumstance, an ancient race-car driver, the death of a peacock at Flannery O'Connor's Andalusia, and, of course, the death of Daniel Wallace's chicken.

The only things these stories have in common are the region they come from and drive of every writer to help us understand our South in all its complexities, paradoxes, and dualities, so that we might, over the long haul, bring about a better South.

We hope you enjoy this volume.

FOREWORD

First Published August 20, 2013

With Drawl

❖❖❖

LAURA RELYEA

Any Southerner with a drawl or a twang in the voice is subject to derision, particularly when we venture outside our region. Folks hear the accent and the conclusions come quickly, even if they're unspoken: We're stupid. We're slow. We're backward. That's why the work of N.C. State professor Walt Wolfram matters so much. He's made it his mission to preserve the languages and dialects of the South. Today, writer Laura Relyea presents a great celebration and fierce defense of our twangs.

I began to lose my Southern accent on U.S. Highway 74 in December 1995, strapped into the bucket seats of my parents' turquoise minivan. We were moving from Charlotte, N.C., to Chicago. I was 10.

I had seen snow only once — a dusting and ice storm that struck the Southeast in the winter of '92, an inch of powder that stuck to the ground for a day. Ice clung heavily to the branches of barren trees. My parents dressed my sister and me in several layers of clothing (we didn't have much in the way of winter coats at the time) and sent us outside to play. We made snow angels. We threw snowballs. The whole world shut down that day. It was just Sarah and me, our cold, sniffly red noses outside, and then inside, hovered over hot cocoa, waiting for our faces to thaw.

When our parents told us we were moving to the suburbs of Chicago we could barely contain our excitement. Not only would we be city girls soon — but the thought of the endless snow fights and raillery that awaited us filled us with thrills. And sure, the Charlotte Hornets were great (Muggsy Bogues! Larry Johnson!) but the Chicago Bulls were even better (Michael Jordan!). Undoubtedly our move to Chicago would be a comparable step toward our own greatness.

Our father preceded us to the city in late November, and we followed him up in early December, just in time for Christmas.

The real shock of our move wasn't the weather at all.

Within a day or two of our arrival my mother marched Sarah and me to the library to register for library cards. I held open the door for a woman who arrived alongside us, she breezed through without acknowledging my mother, my sister or me.

"Mah-ma," I whispered, "she didn't say thank you." The woman turned on her heel and pointed her finger in my face. "I would never say thank you to a child." She sneered at me — a puffy-faced kid with watering eyes.

The stage was set.

School started not long after. My teacher introduced me to the class, told them I was from Charlotte. The class was diverse: Filipino, African-American, Caucasian, Polish. But Southern? Not one, save me. The interrogations and accusations felt close to immediate, especially when I opened my mouth.

"She must be racist," they said.

They called me stupid — slow. It didn't matter I was in advanced classes or was nerdily bookish. It didn't matter that a good number of my best friends in Charlotte had been black. Race wasn't something that occurred to me on the red-clay playgrounds of Charlotte. In Chicago they wouldn't let me forget it.

My Old Piedmont drawl pigeonholed me, and there was no relief in sight, until it occurred to me: Lose the accent.

And that's precisely what I set about doing.

For months I didn't speak in class unless called upon. Mostly I kept to myself and sat in the back, hovered over my textbooks, listening. At lunch I fumbled with my bubble packet of milk, ate my turkey sandwich and studied the way my classmates spoke: "ruff," not roof; "pop," not Coke or Co' cola; "Mom," not Mama. Each linguistic sacrifice pained me, but if I was going to make a life for myself in Chicago, I had to assimilate.

As an adult I've learned that being Southern isn't just about a hometown or an accent — it's a state of mind. It's an assumption that the tea will be sweet; that the bulk of the year will be passed with a thin film of salt on your skin; that our histories come with a distinct sordidness that's better to embrace and grow from than deny. But the truth remains:

With the sacrifice of our language, we begin to sacrifice our culture and identity.

Now, when people ask me where my hometown is I am left perplexed. I could never quite get comfortable in the Midwest, though over time it grew on me. My longing for the Southeast was unerring, but I can't claim it. After college graduation I came South, this time to Atlanta. I've been here now nearly seven years — longer than I've ever lived anywhere — but I'm still unsure if the region would call me one of its own. Why? Because I simply don't sound the part.

But what would I have sounded like with my drawl? What does a North Carolinian sound like?

I began an odyssey to find the answer to that question. It led me on a direct path to a man named Walt Wolfram.

DR. WOLFRAM

Walt Wolfram doesn't sound his part, either. He has spent the bulk of his career defending the Southern accent, but he's from Philadelphia, Pennsylvania.

"I've got this trick," he says. "If I'm doing a talk for a group of Carolinians and one of them calls me out for my own accent, I tell them yes, I'm from Pittsburgh, but eight of my 12 grandchildren are born and raised North Carolinians — and hope to be lifelong residents — and I couldn't be more proud of that. They usually applaud." He laughs at himself, something he does often.

At first glance Wolfram is intimidating — a towering 6-feet-plus patriarch. But once he opens his mouth it's clear that there are few men on earth more congenial and gregarious. I'd have never guessed he was 74 if he hadn't told me; his energy is much younger than that.

"My father worked until he was 82, and it gave him a reason for living," he says. "I figure I'll follow suit. I don't know what I would do with myself without my work."

Wolfram grew up the son of two German immigrants — and as a result was no stranger to linguistic discrimination as he grew up. A German accent wasn't exactly welcomed in the America of the 1940s and '50s. As a result he rarely spoke German at home with his parents, opting instead to assimilate fully with English.

Wolfram's original ambition was to become a missionary — a pursuit he followed through Wheaton College, where he got his bachelor's in 1963. But at the Hartford Seminary Foundation, Wolfram's path crossed with Roger Shuy, the man who would become his mentor.

His work within Shuy's linguistic studies program took Wolfram to Detroit in 1966 where he studied African-American dialects of English. His time within the city would prove critical later in his career: When the Oakland Unified School District stirred up social controversy in late 1996 by passing legislation recognizing African-American English — commonly referred to as "ebonics" — as a legitimate language. Wolfram rose to the statute's defense against much opposition, using findings from his endless research in the area to support it, citing the complex patterns and vocabulary of the dialects he and his fellow researchers had documented.

By then though, Wolfram had already moved to North Carolina, with his wife Marge. After teaching at Georgetown and the University of the District of Columbia, and working as the director of research for the Center for

Applied Linguistics for 12 years, Wolfram joined the faculty of North Carolina State University as the William C. Friday Distinguished University Professor of English Linguistics in 1992. It was the move to the state that led him to the second love of his life: the state of North Carolina itself.

A LINGUIST'S HEAVEN

"I died and went to dialect heaven!" is a phrase you're very likely to hear in conversation with Wolfram. He says it readily and often — in publications, presentations and interviews — because he means it.

In his two decades at N.C. State, Wolfram, his students and fellow members of the North Carolina Language and Life Project (NCLLP), which Wolfram founded, have collected more than 2,500 interviews with North Carolinians. These interviews have yielded multiple books, including Talkin' Tarheel — the first book to ever incorporate over 100 audio recordings into an interactive text — 11 different documentary films exploring varieties of Southern English throughout the state and an endless number of articles. Wolfram himself has produced more than 20 books and 300 articles in his career.

As impressive as this all is, it may also sound pretty highfalutin and academic. But the real difference that the NCLLP has made has been within the communities themselves.

"Linguistic discrimination is the most socially acceptable form of discrimination in the United States," Wolfram told me during our first phone interview this past July. His work is focused on debunking the misperceptions we make based on dialect — by educating and spreading their knowledge through the documentaries they make, by speaking publicly and developing museum and cultural center installations to help spread awareness.

But what makes North Carolina itself so transfixing to a linguist? First and foremost, Wolfram cites the endless diversity of the state — and not just ethnically, though the state is certainly not lacking in racial diversity. Geographically, the state has it all: mountain regions, plains and a vast coast. The state boasts ever-developing urban meccas in Charlotte, Greensboro and Raleigh, as well as a vast number of small towns and rural areas. Socioeconomically, the state is robust and developing, with a wide range of active industries functioning within it — from the second largest banking capital in the United States in Charlotte, to the tobacco and textile industries scattered throughout its landscape.

"Along with the great diversity there's a lot of state pride, and Southern pride," Wolfram says. "The people who have lived here all their lives tend to love this state, which isn't as characteristic of Northern states. North Carolinians have been coached into really treasuring their state — the vegetation, the cultural groups. We're proud of our poets, our writers, our musicians. When you're in a state that really likes itself, it's easier to work within."

Wolfram has made it his agenda to add language and dialect to that long list of things to love.

The geographic makeup of certain regions has caused a few gems, linguistic petri dishes, to develop over the centuries, especially in the state's more remote areas — most specifically Ocracoke Island on the Outer Banks and the Appalachian mountains, most specifically. These are places where the influence of Scots-Irish immigrants from the early 1800s can still be heard loud and clear.

It's no surprise that it was interactions with N.C. State students from Appalachia which led to the founding of the founding of the NCLLP in the first place. Studies conducted by Stephany B. Dunstan as well as by Lauren Hall-Lew and Nola Stephens found that students from the region had to deal with a number of different reactions to their accents throughout their college experience. They were at times patronized and antagonized not only by their peers but also by faculty and university employees as well. Even within the safety of their own state they were presumed to be simple and slow — hicks or hillbillies. Wolfram made it his agenda to adjust people's perceptions of the region, and there was no better way than by going straight to the source.

MOUNTAIN TALK

Many people, when they think of a "hillbilly," might imagine someone much like Marvin "Popcorn" Sutton — a bona fide moonshining Appalachian native who often sported a limp fedora, a long beard that would make members of ZZ Top envious, overalls and flannel shirt. It's true that during his time Popcorn became almost a living archetype of his region. He, along with multiple members of his community, are showcased in the NCLLP's documentary "Mountain Talk."

The mountains of western North Carolina brim with personality. It's a place where you don't carry a bag — you carry a poke; where anything lopsided is "sigogglin"; where red fox squirrels are "boomers"; and well-intentioned out-oftowners such as myself are "jaspers," — so long as they don't settle down there for half the year in retirement, else they be "halfbacks."

Though the U.S. Geological Survey defines 13 Appalachian provinces across the states, culturally speaking the region ranges from northern Georgia as far north as Pennsylvania, encompassing West Virginia and everything between: portions of Georgia, Tennessee, North Carolina, South Carolina and Kentucky.

The word "hillbilly" made its debut in the modern American lexicon on April 23, 1900, in the New York Medical Journal, which defined it as "a free and untrammeled white citizen of Alabama who lives in the hills, has no means to speak of, dresses as he can, talks as he pleases, drinks whiskey when he gets it, and fires off his revolver as the fancy takes him" — not exactly a becoming portrait. These days most folks hear the word "hillbilly and immediately think of "Deliverance" and the eerie melody of "Dueling Banjos" or "The Beverly Hillbillies." (In some social circles, we're lucky enough to think of Andy Griffith.)

But Popcorn and the stars of NCLLP's "Mountain Talk" and "The Queen Family" embrace the term. To them, it's a badge of honor — a slight that's emblematic of their way of life.

"We are 20 years behind the whole country. But I wouldn't swap places with nobody. I feel much more comfortable here being 20 years behind everybody than I would be a-sittin' in a lot of other places and being so miserable. You don't like your neighbor. You don't speak to your neighbor. You're bitter with the world. Atlanta is a good example, or Raleigh. You drive down the street and everybody is wide open blowing their horns and don't know nobody and don't want to know nobody and don't care about nobody. It's quite a bit different up here."

BEFORE YOU KNOW IT, IT AIN'T THE SAME

When I moved back to the South — to Atlanta — there were few things I hoped for more than the return of my Southern accent. But much to my chagrin, the twang and drawl I longed to hear was seldom found in the city — despite living in what's considered to be "the Deep South." A hard fact became clear to me: Native Atlantans might as well be unicorns. Wolfram assures me, it's much the same case in the urban areas of North Carolina.

The day 'y'all' first resurfaced in my vocabulary was a triumphant one. It was a Saturday, and I was stuck in the traffic Atlanta is so notorious for; my temper was put to the test. Driving to the DeKalb Farmers Market was worse than swimming in cold waters upstream. After being cut off a handful of times I angrily wagged my finger in the air and shouted a few choice expletives. But amidst them, there it was, rolling off my tongue naturally: "all y'all." My anger vanished immediately. I was overjoyed. The next thing I yelled was simply: "Oh my gosh! I said y'all! I said y'all!"

Sure — any Yankee or non-native could say y'all. In fact, many of them do. But that's beside the point. For that one, shining moment, I felt like I had reclaimed a part of myself that had been sitting in the back of my closet covered in cobwebs since 1995. Despite the fact that twangs are few and far between in the urban sprawl of Atlanta, for one joyous moment I had mine again. As for instinctively omitting my R's and gliding around my I's, it's still a work in progress.

Atlanta is not alone in growing estranged from its dialect. The change can be felt even in the region's more remote areas. Language is ever-evolving — and the changes are speeding up exponentially over the past century. It seems that with every development comes a cultural sacrifice. The major highway systems connect us, but have had a momentous impact on the disappearance of the small town. The introduction of the air conditioner in 1902 may have cooled our brows, but it also took us off of our porches and indoors, not to mention acclimating the environment enough for Northerners/Yankees to migrate down with much more comfort.

At what point is accommodation a sacrifice?

Though it would take a lot for the Southern accent to disappear completely, the combination of the negative stereotypes that accompany a strong twang, along with the influx of non-natives from all over the world to urban areas, is causing the language to change rapidly. Few have articulated this as well as Martha Pearl Villas, a Charlottean cooking show host.

A century ago, less than 15 percent of North Carolina could be considered "urban," whereas today more than 60 percent of North Carolina's residents live in urban areas. And though saying "y'all" has never been trendier, there's no use denying what's been made clear — the more urban our populations become, the more we lose our drawls.

IT COMES FROM A GOOD PLACE

"Everyone has an instinct to celebrate where they're from, where they were raised," says Wolfram. "We've got this need to come from good places. Southern dialect is part of that heritage — our society is so discriminatory that it's disguised that fact."

On a sunny September day in Raleigh, I met with Walt in his office at N.C. State prior to a talk he was giving, reviewing his work in Appalachia. Walt's office is impeccably professorial — shining mahogany furniture, plants and books everywhere, a hint of coffee in the air. Students milled in and out as we spoke, gathering research items from his bookshelves, popping in to discuss their findings. They're devoted to him and their work, it's immediately clear. A number of his students would spend a portion of the next week at the North Carolina State Fairgrounds, conducting interviews and spreading the awareness of their work, and rallying folks to share their stories of being misunderstood or judged for how they sound.

"It happens every time I give a talk," Wolfram tells me. "People come up afterward to tell me about their own accents, or the way they've been mistreated." He tells me the first step in correcting this discrimination is raising awareness. "As one of my colleagues has said, language prejudice is the last prejudice that is completely tolerated in our society — and it leaves the back door to discrimination wide open.

"We're so tolerant of language prejudice — people can manifest other kinds of prejudice by picking on the language. Northerners who don't like Southern speech basically don't like Southerners, and their speech is an emblem of that. Or in some cases, I had a black friend in Washington, D.C., who hated Southern speech, and the reason she hated it was because she had grown up in the South and experienced a lot of prejudice. Southern speech was sort of the symbol of that. In a sense, voice projects other behavioral traits. It's a precursive thing where one thing triggers another. "

The scope of the North Carolina Language and Life Project, and Wolfram's work, is expanding. Currently his students are being dispatched all around the country — Detroit, Atlanta and everywhere in between — conducting sociolinguistic studies within African-American communities. It's their philosophy that, especially in the current racial environment, this work isn't just significant — it's critical. Walt's work in supporting the Oakland Unified School District was just the beginning. To this day, ill-founded assumptions are made about intellect and social value based only on the sound of one's voice. Wolfram and his colleagues are doing everything within their power to change that: talk by talk, recording by recording, presentation by presentation.

WHAT WE RISK LOSING

Multiple languages are lost every year.

The fight to salvage what's left of an endangered language can be quite the uphill battle. Few examples of this are quite as harrowing as that of the Wampanoag and Cherokee communities that remain in the Southeast.

Being repeatedly cast out of their home country throughout the colonization of North America, then all but completely displaced with the Indian Removal Act of 1830, certainly took an irreparable cultural toll on both the Cherokee and Wamaponaug.

The NCLLP's most recent documentary, "First Language," documents the Eastern Cherokees' efforts to retain their language despite the dwindling numbers of fluent speakers in their ranks.

"In the beginning there were only — I'll say 1,200 — of our people escaped The Trail of Tears removal. All of those people spoke the Cherokee language in those days — all 1,200 of them. Today we have 14,000, and only 200 speak the language," says Jerry Wolfe, Beloved Man of the Eastern Cherokee. His numbers are all estimates, but they're accurate.

"I think we might be it," says Cynthia Grant, a fluent Cherokee speaker and community language supervisor at the Kituwah Preservation & Education Center. The Eastern Cherokees are working hard to preserve their languages. Educational programming that happens there, as well as at the Atse Kituwah Immersion Academy, aims to get Cherokee children speaking the language at a young enough age that they can grow up comfortably within it, and pass the along to generations to follow. They also aim to instill the children with the a strong sense of cultural pride.

"Many Indians in America do not have their own language," Grant says in Cherokee at the onset of "First Language." "They have lost it all. I heard about one group of Indians — one woman was the only speaker, but she had a dog. She taught her dog the language and the dog understood. Is that what is going to happen to us?"

Just a few generations ago, Cherokee was the predominant language used in the community. But in the '50s and '60s, things changed.

"When I started school I did not speak English, I only spoke Cherokee," says one tribe member. "The keeper of the school would punish us if we did not speak English. If we spoke Cherokee he would paddle us." Dozens of stories just like this can be heard throughout the film — speaking their own language was banned in the schoolyard. And in just a few generations the population of fluent Cherokee dwindled to less than 300.

Teaching the next generation of Cherokee is no small challenge, especially when the bulk of them come from homes without native speakers — but the community persists hopefully. A similar Lazarus story is taking place in the Wampanoag community, whose language hadn't been spoken fluently for a century — until now.

WHAT AN ACCENT DOES

We're sitting in Walt's office discussing linguistic profiling, such as this example: A white couple makes an inquiry to an apartment complex and schedules a showing, a black couple calls a few minutes later and suddenly, there are no vacancies. And this isn't just an issue for Southerners. What about the Middle Eastern immigrant who takes a phone interview and doesn't get the job?

The whole country needs an attitude adjustment. We need to actively think about the judgements we make when we hear someone. We need to really hear one another.

"My feeling is that it's a social cause," Wolfram says. "My feeling is that if what I do academically has implications for social and linguistic inequality then I have an obligation to address those." Wolfram coined a term for this — linguistic gratuity — some time ago. It's a philosophy that he's acted upon every step of his life. In some ways, he's become both a linguist and the missionary that he set out to become in the '60s, but instead of spreading the good word, he's spreading the goodness of speech.

The NCLLP's research with Appalachian students led to N.C. State incorporating anti-linguistic discrimination curriculum into its orientation programming. It's taught to students, employees and faculty annually. Since its introduction the program has also been picked up by North Carolinian public schools, encouraging students to think of their speech patterns as their cultural identity –something to take pride in.

Here, the late Bill Friday — who was at the helm of the University of North Carolina system for 30 years — discusses the importance of Southern drawl.

With work on the NCLLP's forthcoming documentary series, "Talking Black in America," Wolfram is using a three-year grant to take up the cause of speaking in defense of Black English. His goals are to work with his videographers and develop a series of five or six documentaries on the subject — exploring as many aspects of the culture as possible. His students are recording political figures as well as rap competitions. They're interviewing people on the street and elbowing their way to African-American celebrities with a story and experience to share.

"I really feel like it's necessary to get this message out on a national level," Wolfram says.

He's right — linguistic discrimination is universal: It's what I experienced in moving to Chicago; it's what he experienced growing up as the son of German immigrants; it's what most ESL people undergo as they acclimate to our culture; it's what the Cherokee and Wamaponaug endured when they were taught to believe their native tongue was somehow inferior to English.

My own Southern accent may never come back fully. But Walt Wolfram and the NCLLP led me to realize is that my language is mine. Just like any other part of me, it is the sum of my experiences. It will only continue to evolve.

I'll simply stake my claim in the red clay I call home and hope to be bettered by its influence — to celebrate the sounds around me, all of them.

— Laura Relyea's essays, reviews, poems, and features have also been published in Oxford American, Thought Catalog, Monkey Bicycle, Necessary Fiction, and elsewhere. She is based in Athens, Georgia.

First Published September 10, 2013

The Ghosts of Ponce de Leon Park

•••

FRED WILLARD

A NOTE FROM THE EDITOR

There is, in every city of some size, "a street of appetites" — a place where people with hungers congregate, a street where things happen in dark places. In Atlanta, The Bitter Southerner's hometown, that street has always been Ponce de Leon Avenue. Ponce, as we call it, is home to the legendary Clermont Lounge, where strippers whose average age is 46.5 shake their moneymakers, and the Majestic Diner, which has been serving hangover prevention and cures 24/7 since 1929. Ponce always begs to be the setting of a novel.

Back in 1997, an Atlanta writer named Fred Willard delivered a great one. "Down on Ponce" was hard-boiled crime fiction, solidly in the tradition of Raymond Chandler and Jim Thompson.

"Down on Ponce" permanently planted itself in my brain. I was 36 years old when it came out, and I've gone back to reread it several times. For a guy like me, who loves crime fiction written with verve and feistiness, "Down on Ponce" was just the ticket, particularly because I knew its setting like the back of my hand.

But in the last decade or so, the literary world hasn't seen much of Fred Willard's work. Then a few weeks ago, out of the blue, Willard sent The Bitter Southerner *a short story. The Ghosts of Ponce de Leon Park" is the only work of fiction in this volume.*

THE GHOSTS OF
PONCE DE LEON PARK

"We can thumb some more or just walk down the railroad tracks to Ponce," Bob said.

"My legs don't feel so good," Del said. "The doctors at the clinic said my circulation is bad."

"I know, man. You already told me. Maybe walking will get your circulation going."

"Maybe so. I don't know about that. I just know my legs don't feel good."

Del looked down the rail bed. A tree line on either side hid it from the apartments and the shopping center and as the line curved gently in the distance to the left it also hid the destination.

"How far is it," he asked.

"Maybe a mile."

"I guess we might as well walk it. We might stand around that long waiting for a ride."

They walked between the rails matching strides to the wooden ties.

"I don't know if I can keep this up," Del said.

"We can slow down."

"It ain't the speed it's the reach."

"The gravel's harder."

"I'm going to walk over to the side on the dirt," Del said. He stepped over to the worn path on the edge of the right of way.

"It's softer here," he said.

"That's your problem," Bob said. "You're too damn soft. It's like you never worked."

"I worked plenty."

"Down there is where the snakes are," Bob said.

"I don't see any damn snakes."

Del was slowly falling behind Bob's strides on the railroad ties.

"Hold on. What's the damn hurry?"

"You're in bad shape."

"It's the circulation. The doctors said I might get gangrene. Then they'd have to cut my legs off."

"That's the other thing, your circulation. I can tell you hadn't been working, not without any circulation. So where did you get that stash of money?"

"I ain't got that much."

"But where did you get it? You been sucking dicks?"

"Why did you go and say something like that?"

"Well have you?"

"Hell, no."

"Where did you get the money, then?"

"Sold blood."

"No wonder you can't walk."

"You never sold blood?"

"I never been in bad shape like you are."

"So if I'm in bad shape, why don't you just slow down? It ain't polite running off like that."

"I'll slow down. but this cut-through scares the hell out of me sometimes."

"Why's that?"

"All sorts of bad shit happens back here. The skinheads catch you and they kick your ass. They killed a couple homeless along these tracks. Stomped this one guy till his heart exploded."

"Now you're frightening me. What do they do — hide in the trees till you come by?"

"No. They just use it as a cut-through. They walk over from Little Five Points, go up to Piedmont Park to beat queers. Keep your eyes open. We see anybody, we can get off the tracks and hide. I just don't like thinking about it."

"You wouldn't run off and leave me, if you saw the skinheads coming, would you?"

"I don't know, man. There wouldn't be much point in my sticking around for an ass-whipping if I couldn't do nothing, would there?"

"I'll try to walk faster, but my legs are killing me. If we see some skinheads, help me hide in the trees before you run off."

"I'll do that, Del."

The track had been following a gentle curve, but as it straightened they could see Ponce de Leon Avenue ahead.

"It isn't that much further," Bob said.

They didn't talk as they tried to make time. Del's legs felt raw. They were swelling and he walked with them stiff in a fast shuffle so he could keep up. He counted steps to help the time pass. When they were almost to Ponce he said, "My legs are no good, I got to lay down."

"We farted around so long we can't get nothing at the Open Door or St. Luke's," Bob said. "I guess we might as well spend the night in this kudzu field. You want to buy us both a dinner since we missed it because of your damn circulation."

"You can get us dinner and a couple pints of sherry," Del said.

They walked to the kudzu-covered field to the right of the tracks, and found a little depression where they wouldn't be as visible and unrolled their bedrolls. Del pulled some money out of his stash and handed it to Bob.

"Why don't you take a water bottle."

"Okay, I got to go to Green's then up to the Zesto, so it's going to take me some time, so just hang on."

"I ain't going nowhere," Del said.

NORMAL BOB

When it came down to it, Del didn't know jack-shit about Bob. He thought Bob could just as easy take off with the money and not come back, buy himself a decent dinner and keep all the wine for himself. He had the look of someone who knew how to take care of himself, all right. His jeans, work shirt and heavy shoes were a lot newer than Del's, whose clothes looked like they were about to rot off. Not that he cared anymore, but Del thought they smelled like it too.

At the shelter in Nashville, Bob had got hung with the name Normal Bob. He wasn't so damn normal, but he had the good luck to show up after Crazy Bob who got his instructions from a dog named Tick that nobody else could see. Mostly the dog told him to howl. So Bob became Normal Bob to tell him apart from Crazy Bob.

Normal Bob was going back to Atlanta so Del planned to tag along. Del had a little stash of money and Normal knew the city so it seemed like a good partnership.

Del laid out in his bedroll and put his head on his little bag of clothes and watched the puffy white clouds drift across the early evening sky. In a little while, the night would unzip its bag of tricks and spill the predators into the hundreds of pockets of darkness along this street of appetites, and by then Del hoped to be fed, drunk and sleeping unnoticed among the weeds.

Now that he'd got the weight off his legs, he noticed he was getting the shakes in his hands, but there wasn't nothing he could do about it till Bob got back with the wine. He lay like this about an hour, till twilight, when he heard a man approaching, looked up and saw Bob carrying a couple of sacks.

"I got us both a Chubby Decker Plate."

He handed Del a pint bottle. Del broke the seal, and took three or four gulps, and fought to keep them down. He didn't want to waste any of it.

"You going to eat anything with that?" Bob asked.

"First things first," Del said.

"You shouldn't have made this trip. It was too much for you," Bob said.

"Had to leave Nashville."

"It must have been big trouble," Bob said.

"No, I just wore out my welcome too many places. Life was getting too hard."

"Well, a lot of little trouble can be just as bad as big trouble," Bob said. "Tomorrow morning we can head up to St. Luke's for breakfast. Talk to the guys there. See what's going on."

"I don't know if I can make it," Del said. "I don't think I'm going to be able to walk at all."

"I can call the Grady wagon then, they can take you to the hospital."

"I'm afraid they might have to cut my legs off."

Bob tried to change the subject.

"This place we're sitting is historic. It's the back end of the old Ponce de Leon Baseball Park. That magnolia tree would have been at dead center field. The Atlanta Crackers used to play here. I came to the games with my old man. They tore the place down when they built the new stadium for the Braves. Turned it into this parking lot."

"I never liked this place none," Del said.

"You been here then?"

"I lived in Atlanta a couple months when I was a kid. I came here with my father once," Del said. "What do they call that building across the street?"

"That would be the old Sears and Roebuck. It's got city offices now, so they call it City Hall East."

"I remember the Sears and Roebuck, you got of the trolley and walked across the street to the park."

"That's right, man, they still had the old electric trolleys when the Crackers played here."

"I never had no luck here. We shouldn't have stopped here."

"Hell, you were the one who wanted to stop, Del. You said

your legs were bad. You never should have left Nashville with your legs like that."

"I know that, now," Del said. The memory of the old ball park pinned him to the ground like a stack of cement blocks on his chest.

THE BALL GAME

He woke up in the middle of the night breaking a fever. There was a bright full moon.

"I got to pee bad, man, and I can't move my legs," he said. "I need help getting up."

Bob didn't answer so he pushed himself up a little bit on an elbow and saw the ground where Bob had been sleeping and had crushed the kudzu, but Bob and his bedroll were gone. Del felt for his money stash and it was gone, too. At least he left one of the pints.

There wasn't nothing he could do but lie there until somebody came along to help. He held the pee as long as he could then wet the bed. It felt uncomfortable as it soaked his pants and ran up his back. He didn't think he could go back to sleep, but that wasn't the worst part. Something much more frightening was happening because time was messing up somehow and he was also back in his parents' little shack they had rented in West Atlanta when he was nine years old.

"I was thinking about taking the boy to a ball game," his father said.

Del pretended he wasn't paying attention but he hoped his mother would say yes. She was the one who had a job, and she always watched every penny she made. That's what his parents always fought about.

"I guess we ought to do something for him," his mother said. She walked back to her bedroom, where she kept her money, and closed the door so nobody could hear her hiding place. When she came out she handed a couple folded dollar bills to his father, and some change, too.

"Why don't y'all get yourself a hot dog? That way I don't have to cook nothing for you tonight."

She went back to her room and laid down. She worked so much she was always tired. Some days she went to bed as soon as she got home from work.

After a while his father said, "Okay, boy, it's time to go to that ball game."

He followed his father up to the trolley stop, trying to keep up with his funny bobbing walk. They sat on a hard bench for a few minutes till the trolley came.

"Mr. Driver, I need a transfer for me and my boy." He said it like they always did things together.

The driver tore off two scraps of paper, and handed them to him, and then his father made a big to do about handing one to Del.

"Now you hold onto this, Son. It's what makes you able to ride the second trolley."

They both sat down.

"I like this sideways seat the best," his father explained.

"Me too, " Del agreed.

After a few minutes his father pulled the cord that rang the bell and said, "Time to get off."

They were at another bus stop and Del sat on a bench like the other one.

"Now you sit here, till I get back. No matter what happens, just stay there."

He crossed the street and went in a liquor store and when he came out Del could see a bottle stuck in his front pants pocket. When he sat next to Del he took it out, and held it to his lips and swallowed three or four times.

"Here. You want some?"

He handed it to Del who took a sip but thought it tasted sour, like puke. He pretended to like it, though.

"Here comes the bus." His father put the bottle back in his pants.

"They don't like you to drink this stuff on the bus," he father explained.

Once they got on it seemed like they were at a party.

"Anybody going to see the Crackers?" his father asked.

A bunch of people laughed like his father had told a joke.

"Seems like most of us are," a woman said.

"Have a seat, son."

He sat Del down in the sideways seat, then walked back four or five rows to where there was a bunch of men sitting. He said something, they laughed, and a couple of them looked up toward the driver, then the bottle came out and they were passing it around.

Del looked out the window and watched the people on the street until they stopped next to this big brick building with a tower on top like a castle.

"That's the Sears and Roebuck."

A woman sitting next to him said this when she saw him looking at the building.

"Everybody off the bus," his father said. The men with him laughed like this was pretty funny.

People were already starting to line up to buy tickets, so his father ran ahead and bought two seats in the white bleachers. They went up this ramp into the park and he followed his father and the other men under the wooden seats to a refreshment stand where a man was cooking hot dogs on a grill.

Dell asked, "You going to get us some hot dogs, daddy?"

"Don't have no money left," he said. "But wait a minute here. I got something in my pocket."

He reached in his pocket and pulled out his white handkerchief. He bent down on one knee, and laid it out like a neat square, then stepped back and started doing a little dance like a buck and wing and giving out these little yelps.

He was pretty good at it, but Del didn't like to watch.

Pretty soon a crowd had gathered and people were dropping nickels and dimes, even a few quarters on the handkerchief.

"Thank you very much, folks." his father said. He scooped up the money and handed Del a quarter.

"You keep this in case you need it. Don't spend it on food or nothing. Just hold onto it. Now go on up and get us our seats and I'll be along in a little while."

The men from the bus had gathered around his father again and Del knew he wanted to drink with them, so he went to get their seats in the bleachers. A boy his own age tried to sit down next to him, but he held his hand out over the seat and said, "My daddy's going to be sitting there," so the boy moved over a space.

Pretty soon the teams took to the field and everybody cheered. Del didn't know much that was going on but he acted like he did, so nobody would think he was stupid. He didn't know how to play ball. His parents moved around so he never really got to have many friends and the few boys he knew didn't have the equipment. Still, it was real beautiful to watch. The lights made the field seem bright green and the uniforms stuck out like a cartoon in the newspaper. Out in the distance there was this dirt bank covered with kudzu and a big magnolia tree and over to the right, a railroad track. It didn't look like how he'd imagined a ballpark, but he liked it.

He actually started figuring out the game, at least part of it, and he'd get excited with every pitch, and cheer with the crowd when the players from Birmingham would swing at a pitch and miss.

He was having fun until he figured out that his father wasn't coming to his seat, and then he only watched the game because he knew he ought to be having fun since he probably wasn't going to get to come back.

The Crackers won. As the crowd left, he didn't see his father and he knew he wasn't here. In his pocket, he felt the quarter and wondered if this was the time he was supposed to save the money for, or if there would be another one. Finally he decided this must be the time, because spending it was the only way he was going to get home.

"I'd like a transfer, Mr. Driver." he said

The man gave him a funny look, but handed him the transfer.

Del was pretty sure he could spot the street where he lived, but he wasn't too sure about the stop by the liquor store, so he sat in the sideways seat twisted around with his face pressed against the window. It turned out to be easy to see because of the lights, so he rang the bell and got off the trolley.

He was quiet going in the house. He was starving and got a piece of bread. He hoped his mother wouldn't notice and get mad.

"That you boy?" she called from the bedroom.

"Yes ma'am."

"Is your father with you?"

"No ma'am, he ain't."

"I should have known," she said. "He don't care nothing about you. He just wanted the money so he could get a drink."

"He won't be coming back neither," she said. "I told him the next time he took to drinking he couldn't come back, but sometimes that man needs a drink so bad he'd trade his whole life for it."

A NEW BODY

Del woke up, or he thought he woke up. It seemed like he was back in the kudzu field and there were men standing around him, but something reminded him of the mission back at Nashville.

It was the picture the reverend had taken him aside to see. Some old drunk had painted it from the Book of Revelation showing skeletons on winged horses, the four horsemen of the apocalypse riding above the battle field at Armageddon. He hadn't understood then what the preacher had meant, showing it to him like that, but now he knew that he had been shown his death.

He might as well have put his hands on Del's head in benediction and said, "Go forth my son, and die by skinhead," because Del knew the four men looking down at him were going to kill him. They didn't have any hair and their skin was stretched tight and showed their skulls. The moonlight made it seem they had bleached bone instead of flesh and their eyes had retreated in their sockets. They leaned over Del lying in his bedroll and his own piss.

"He smells rank," one of the men said.

"Let's put him out of his misery."

"It's my legs," Del said. "They ain't no good."

"Don't worry old man. God's going to give you a new body."

Del saw the heel of the boot coming down on his face, felt bone crunching, and heard a sound like loud ringing in his ears. He let go of everything and didn't know nothing they did after that.

Del was unconscious and then he saw the kudzu in front of his face again. There was a man standing next to him. The man knelt down and put his hand on Del's shoulder.

"Hello, son. I've been wanting to talk to you for a long time."

Del knew he was dead because it was his father's voice. He stood up quickly, held his arm in front of him and marveled at it. It was milky white under the full moon and had perfect skin like a baby's, like he had never worked in the sun or fallen down.

The dark green kudzu was silver where it was kissed by the light and his father's face was beautiful like a blessing Del had never seen in this world.

"I've been wanting to tell you that I always loved you. I didn't leave you that night, and that's the truth. Some bad men took me away from the ball park in their automobile. They took me out of town and killed me. They cut my gut open so my body wouldn't float, and they wrapped me in burlap, and tied cement blocks to me, and they threw me in the Chattahoochee River. I swear, son, that I never meant to leave you that night. I always loved you. And now I've been sent down here to take you up to heaven," he said.

Del picked up the bottle, took a little sip and saw the hunger on his father's face as he looked at the sherry. He wouldn't offer him any. He'd wait for him to ask ... or maybe even beg.

"If you just come from heaven, how come you want a drink so bad?" Del asked.

"They sent me down to get you, son. You don't go with me, you got to stay by yourself."

"You always were a liar. How do I know it's heaven you're taking me to?"

"Could you give me a taste of that wine? Then we could go up there. Don't you want to be with the other people? Your mother's up there."

Del turned around, kicked his dirty bed roll and started walking fast to the railroad, then running down the tracks leaving his father far behind. Now that God have given him his new body, he didn't need nobody or their stinking lies. From now on he would travel alone.

— *Fred Willard is the author of two novels, Down on Ponce and Princess Naughty and the Voodoo Cadillac.*

First Published October 29, 2013

The Whys

•••

LOLIS ERIC ELIE

This Saturday will mark 10 years since the federal levees failed in New Orleans, flooding 80 percent of the city. For two weeks now, we've been seeing "How New Orleans Came Back" stories all over the media. Here at The Bitter Southerner, we were interested in a deeper question: Why did New Orleanians come back and redeem their city after Hurricane Katrina? We asked one of our favorite New Orleans writers, Lolis Eric Elie, to explain it for us.

Some of us came back because we lived in the old city — the Vieux Carre, Faubourg Treme, the Irish Channel, Niggertown, the Marigny, the Garden District, the Warehouse District — the 20 percent of the city that didn't flood.

Some of us came back because we had a cousin or auntie and they said we could stay by them until we got it figured out.

Some of us came back because we knew they didn't want us back.

Some of us came back because we got tired of having to fight just because we were from New Orleans.

Some of us came back because we didn't think it would take that long or cost that much or require so many tears and so many pained laughs to fix just one house.

Some of us came back because we thought we knew for sure we had enough insurance to fix everything.

Some of us came back because we didn't believe that the insurance company that we'd dutifully paid for decades would cheat us in our hour of gravest need.

(If Dante Alighieri had endured the inferno of our flood, he would have kindled a special fire for insurance companies!)

Some of us came back because we know what it means.

Some of us came back because we didn't want to keep saying Hoover or Pittsburgh or Sugarland when somebody asked, "Where y'at?"

Some of us came back because, have you ever been to Kalamazoo?

Some us came back because it didn't flood on our second story and we could live there while they fixed the first.

Some of us came back because we had rebuilding skills.

Some of us came back because Richard Baker, the Baton Rouge Congressman, was right: "We finally cleaned up public housing in New Orleans. We couldn't do it, but God did."

Some of us came back to fight for our homes in the Lafitte, in the Magnolia, in the B.W. Cooper, in the Melpomene, in those timeworn fortresses, those unflooded, moldless bricks.

Some of us came back because the traffic in Baton Rouge was one reason too many to hate that place.

Some of us came back because we had sharpened our clippers and smoothened our tongues and poised ourselves to fleece the sheep, the desperate homeowners begging for help.

Some of us came back because we felt a moral obligation to rebuild our city.

Some of us came back because the arrow of our moral compass points permanently in the direction of steal.

Some of us came back because Yemaya, the orisha of the waters, was true to Her word and protected New Orleans from the brunt of the storm (though it would have been nice if She had told us that the federal levees were not in Her purview).

Some of us came back because we believed Him when He said to us, "Truly I tell you, whatever you did for one of the least of these brothers and sisters of mine, you did for me."

Some of us came back because G-d said, "For the poor will never cease out of the land; therefore I command you, You shall open wide your hand to your brother, to the needy and to the poor, in the land."

Some of us came back because the Prophet (peace be upon Him) promised us in Surah 2:215, "They ask you, [O Muhammad], what they should spend. Say, 'Whatever you spend of good is [to be] for parents and relatives and orphans and the needy and the traveler. And whatever you do of good - indeed, Allah is knowing of it.'"

Some of us were inspired to come back by Rep. Dennis Hastert (may his sentence be a long one). He said our city was seven feet below sea level, and we wished to visit this twisted Atlantis of his dreams.

Some of us came back because, as Pastafarians, we thought the Flying Spaghetti Monster would want us to help in the rebuilding.

Some of us came back because, as bad as things were, we didn't believe the ancestors would ever forgive us for being buried in Texas.

Some of us came back because, if they didn't have enough police to arrest the murderers, they certainly didn't have enough to arrest the fraudsters.

Some of us came back because, even after Bush's boys took their cut, and Cheney's boys took their cut, and the Shaw Group took its cut, there was still enough piss trickling down the leg of the disaster capitalism for us to make us a couple of dollars putting blue tarps on damaged roofs.

Some of us came back because every year, at Carnival time, we make a new suit.

Some of us came back because we're Prince of Wales and we knew if we paraded, even two months late, it would be as a healing balm unto the people.

Some of us came back because, when we saw Prince of Wales Social Aid & Pleasure Club, we knew God was in his heaven and New Orleans was still New Orleans.

Some us came back because of the feeling we got visiting home that first Carnival after Katrina when we saw the people, our people, in the street, being us the way we be us when we gather like we do.

Some of us came back because if we heard one more person pronounce it N'awlins ...

Some of us came back because we'd rather be doing bad in

New Orleans than doing good somewhere else.

Some of us came back because we had promised ourselves, Everything I Do Gon Be Funky From Now On, and that shit didn't even much sound right coming out of your mouth in Topeka.

Some of us came back because we didn't want those lazy Mexicans taking all our jobs.

Some of us came back to prove that we were willing and able to work as hard as any Mexican.

Some of us came back because, just like the Mexicans and the Brazilians and the Hondurans we had to make that rebuilding money to send home to our wives and husbands and children and friends because they were depending on us for their beans and rice.

Some of us came back because there was plenty of copper in those flooded homes, ripe for the stealing.

Some of us came back because we were second story men by profession and there was plenty to steal on unflooded second stories.

Some of us came back because we thought the Saints would never win a Super Bowl if we weren't personally in New Orleans our own self.

Some of us came back because seeing the city depopulated and dirty, desperate and quiet, awakened a patriotism in us.

Some of us came back because we wanted to end our high school career at the same place we'd started it.

Some of us came back because after kicking the French in the ass, and kicking the Americans in the ass, and escaping the sea-born treacheries of the Thai fisherman, rebuilding A Village Called Versailles was a pretty much a piece of mung-bean cake.

Some of us came back because we declined to depend on the kindness of strangers.

Some of us came back because we felt the crusts of bread and such from our rich relations would not long continue.

Some of us came back to give lie to the stereotypes about us.

Some of us came back because the stereotypes about us were true.

Some of us came back because we were angry that a massive federal effort was rebuilding foreign cities laid waste by American ingenuity while an American city laid waste by faulty American engineering was left foundering.

Some of us came back because Sweet Home New Orleans helped us find affordable housing.

Some of us came back because the Foundation for Louisiana helped us re-open our business.

Some of us came back because Seedco Financial helped us reopen our business.

Some of us came back because we got money from Jazz at Lincoln Center's Higher Ground benefit.

Some of us came back because we found a home in Musicians' Village.

Some of us came back because neither the food in Lafayette nor the music in Lafayette could make up for the Lafayette in Lafayette.

Some of us came back because we thought, maybe if we scrubbed hard enough, we could wipe that smirk off of George Bush's face.

Some of us came back because, when we left, we left in a hurry and didn't have time to heed Fran Lebowitz's advice that if you're going to America, you should bring your own food.

(Oh, Mr. Aligheri! If only there had been even a little salt taste in those other men's bread!)

Some of us came back because the New Orleans Musicians' Clinic sponsored gigs for us to play and to pay our bills and support our families.

Some of us came back because we won't bow down. We don't know how.

Some us came back to collect the addresses of the displaced so that we could apply for their federal assistance checks before they knew what time it was.

Some of us came back courtesy of grants from the Soros Open Society Foundation.

Some of us came back because, unlike the Iraqi Americans, we were not allowed to vote long distance in our local elections if we lived outside our home state.

Some of us came back to help re-elect our mayor.

Some of us came back because the only way we could move the city forward was to elect a new mayor.

Some of us came back because the Tipitina's Foundation got us horns for our marching band.

Some of us came back to bear witness.

Some of us came back because our grandfather built this house.

Some of us came back because, I'll be got damn if I'm gonna let my cousins just take this house my grandfather built right from under my nose.

Some of us came back to prevent a land grab.

Some of us came back to grab us some land.

Some of us came back because we got a really good deal on some Stone Age marble.

Some of us came back because you're my piece of the rock and I love you C.C.

All of us came back — like the people of New York after 9-11, like the people of Chile after 9-11, like the people of Vietnam after the American War, like the people of Mississippi after the 1927 flood, like the people of Lisbon after the great earthquake, like the people of Harlan County during the 1931 coal strike, like the people of Indonesia after the great tsunami, like the people of Los Angeles after the Northridge earthquake, like the people of Haiti after paying reparations to the French, like the people of Chicago after the great fire, like the people of Rwanda after the genocide, like the people of Iran after the Eisenhower coup, like the Cherokee after Andrew Jackson, like the people of the Dominican Republic after the American invasion, like the people of Russia after World War II, like the people of Guatemala after the CIA coup, like the people of Cambodia after the Kissinger carpet bombings — because rebuilding our homes and ourselves was our response to Camus' one really serious philosophical question, the question of suicide.

— Lolis Eric Elie is a New Orleans-born, Los Angeles-based writer and filmmaker. Most recently, he joined the writing staff of the Amazon series The Man in the High Castle. Before that, he wrote for the OWN series Greenleaf and the HBO series Treme.

First Published November 26, 2013

How Hot Chicken Really Happened

•••

RACHEL L. MARTIN, PH.D.

Rachel Martin left her hometown for eight years, then returned to find everyone talking about a dish she'd never heard of or eaten in the Nashville of her youth: hot chicken. Today, we learn how Nashville's signature dish stayed hidden for decades in the city's black communities — and then suddenly became a global obsession.

Hot chicken.

It's on the list of "must-try" Southern foods in countless publications and websites. Restaurants in New York, Detroit, Cambridge and even Australia advertise that they fry their chicken Nashville-style. More than 12,000 people showed up for the 2014 Fourth of July Music City Hot Chicken Festival. The James Beard Foundation recently gave Prince's Chicken Shack an American Classic Award for inventing the dish.

But although I'm a second-generation Middle Tennessean, the daughter of a Nashville native, I had never eaten hot chicken — or even heard of it — before I moved away for graduate school in 2005. I came back eight years later to a new Nashville that eats new food.

The city is growing almost faster than developers can manage. Historic neighborhoods are being razed and renewed. The suburbs are expanding. Fields are being replaced by paved shopping paradises identical to those spreading across the nation. My friends have moved to the neighborhoods we grew up avoiding. They asked me to meet them for drinks or haute Southern cuisine in places I remembered as industrial wastelands. And everyone was eating hot chicken, a food I didn't know.

Embarrassed that I didn't know this food everyone else loved, I turned to Google. The web was full of photographs of fried chicken slathered with a hot sauce that somehow kept it crispy, served on a bed of white bread and topped by a pickle. Then last summer, my friend Julie moved home. She called me.

"What's hot chicken?" she asked. "Have we been eating our chicken wrong all these years?"

I asked my dad if he had ever had it. "Nope," he said. But he taught school in the 1970s, and he remembered that some of the black teachers carried their own bottles of hot sauce. Sometimes they'd prank him by spiking his cafeteria lunch.

Was this the answer? Was hot chicken a part of the city's history that had been invisible to me as a white woman?

I asked Denise, an older African-American woman in my church who was raised in the city.

"Of course you didn't eat hot chicken," she said, shaking her head at me. "Hot chicken's what we ate in the neighborhood."

I went to the Downtown Public Library to do a very unscientific survey of what they had on hand. I sat in their second-floor reading room, surrounded by stacks of cookbooks, just to see if I could find a recipe to prove that in Nashville we didn't choose our chicken style based on race. I walked away with several new ways to fry a chicken. One of them added some black pepper, but none of them made it spicy.

Sure enough, as I started investigating, I discovered Denise was right. For almost 70 years, hot chicken was made and sold primarily in Nashville's black neighborhoods. I started to suspect the story of hot chicken could tell me something powerful about race relations in Nashville, especially as the city tries to figure out what it will be in the future.

HOT AS HELL'S HALF ACRE

I hate it when people date everything Southern back to the Civil War. But in this case, that's where my story starts. That is when Nashville became a segregated city, a place where there were white neighborhoods and black neighborhoods and very little shared public space.

Before the war, about 700 free blacks lived in Nashville. Their houses were clustered in small enclaves, mostly on the northern side of the city. But there were over 3,200 enslaved people of color in the city. Most of them could not choose where they lived.

Many enslaved African-Americans used the war to claim their freedom. They left their homes and moved to the edges of Union camps. The places where the freed people lived became known as contraband camps. Some of these were migrant communities following the soldiers as they campaigned. Others were permanent settlements where residents plotted streets, built wood cabins and organized churches.

Federal troops captured Nashville in February 1862. The first Southern state capital to be taken, its early capitulation meant that the city became a key Union base. African-Americans from across Middle Tennessee fled there, and contraband camps sprouted up around the military installations perched on the eastern, western and southern borders of Nashville.

After the Civil War ended, the people living in Nashville's contraband camps had a choice: return to the places they had lived before the conflict, hoping to negotiate new contracts with the whites who once claimed to own them; strike out for somewhere new, gambling that they would find more opportunity in the North or the West; or stay in Nashville, building a new life in the growing city. Many chose to remain. Between 1860 and 1870, African-Americans grew from being 23 to 38 percent of the population.

One of the largest Union camps had been Fort Gillem, north of downtown and near where the free blacks lived before the war. When the Union Army pulled out, Fisk Free Colored School took over the grounds. Rechartered as Fisk University in 1872, it became a leading institution of African-American higher education. The wagon road through the fort was renamed Jefferson Street. A prosperous black business district grew up along it, and houses popped up around it.

Several other large African-American neighborhoods developed around former camps located in what is now known as East Nashville, just across the Cumberland River from downtown. Like the Jefferson Street area, these were neighborhoods filled with professionals, businesspeople and skilled laborers.

Another black neighborhood grew up a few blocks northwest of the state capital. Known as Hell's Half Acre, it housed the poorest African-Americans in the city. It had unpaved streets and no sewer system. The city's disinterest left the area open to trouble. It became known for saloons, prostitution and other vices. It also had some of Nashville's oldest black churches and schools.

IT ALL GOES BACK TO THORNTON

Over the last decade or so, the story of how hot chicken was invented has become part of local mythology, the sort of tale Nashville residents can recount with dramatic pauses and wry chuckles.

It happened this way: Back in the 1930s at the height of the Great Depression, there was a man named Thornton Prince. He was a handsome man, tall and good looking.

"Beautiful, wavy hair," his great-niece Andre Prince Jeffries tells me. He was also a bit of a womanizer. "He was totally a ladies' man," she laughs. "He sure had plenty of women."

Women handle cheating partners in all sorts of ways. Some look the other way. Others walk out. A few get even.

One of Thornton's women got fed up with his philandering ways. He had stayed out all night and come home expecting breakfast. She wanted retribution. That morning, just like all their other morning-afters, she got up before him. And she didn't make him dry toast or gruel. Oh, no, she made him his favorite. She made him fried chicken.

Then, she added the spiciest items she had in her kitchen.

No one knows what went into that first hot chicken. "She couldn't run to the grocery store to get something," Jeffries muses. By the time the bird was cooked, she was sure she had spiced it beyond edibility.

As Thornton Prince took his first bite, she must have braced herself for his reaction. Would he curse? Whimper? Stomp out?

But her plan backfired. He loved it. He took it to his brothers. They loved it, too.

The woman disappeared from his life, but her hot chicken lived on. The Prince brothers turned her idea into the BBQ Chicken Shack.

"We don't know who the lady was that was trying," Jeffries says. "All the old heads are gone. Gone on. But hey, we're still profiting from it." She pauses. "So women are very important."

Jeffries has an easy explanation for the chicken's popularity. "My mother said, if you know people are gonna talk, give them something to talk about," she says. "This chicken is not boring. You're gonna talk about this chicken."

Jeffries tells me this sitting in a bench at Prince's Chicken Shack, the business founded eight decades ago. She is about 70, with carefully applied makeup, a Farrah Fawcett flip and a contagious laugh. She moves a little stiffly, but she's still the one who runs the restaurant. As we talk, she keeps a close eye on her employees, many of whom are either family members or longtime friends.

I'm at Prince's early on a Thursday evening, so most folks are picking up to-go dinner orders. Customers file past our table. Some stop to share their own memories. They walk by us to the back of the restaurant where a plywood wall separates the dining room from the kitchen. A window has been cut in the wall, and a woman sits there, ringing up the orders. Occasionally, she yells a number and hands over a brown paper bag of food. The chicken's grease and sauce quickly saturate the paper, so most customers grab a white plastic bag off a nearby counter. A young man is stapling strands of yellow, white and red Christmas lights around the window.

Of course, a few folks say that before there was Prince's BBQ Chicken Shack, there was a place called Bo's. But who wants to mess with a good story?

TOO FAR DOWN THE PYRAMID

By the time Thornton Prince opened his restaurant, segregation governed Southern life.

Reconstruction had seemed to offer African-Americans new opportunities. Black men got the vote, and a handful were elected. Schools opened, educating children and adults alike. People hoped for land ownership and fair wages. But the abandonment of the federal government and violent opposition by groups such as the Ku Klux Klan let white Southerners "redeem" their communities. Jim Crow laws hardened the divisions between blacks and whites, making inequality part of the legal code. Lynchings, riots, rapes and other attacks terrorized black communities. Many people left the region, hoping Chicago or New York or Los Angeles would be more peaceful and profitable for them. Others fled the countryside for Nashville and the other cities of the upper South.

Jefferson Street gave black Nashvillians places where they could shop, eat, learn and worship safely. Thanks to these new migrants, the area around Jefferson Street continued to grow and prosper. In 1912, the Tennessee Agricultural and Industrial and Normal School — now Tennessee State University — moved there. That same year, the city built Hadley Park, the first park blacks could use. Restaurants, music venues and speakeasies opened. Country music dominated white Nashville's music scene, but Jefferson Street became an important haunt for jazz and blues musicians. The Ritz Theater let African-Americans watch movies without having to climb into a segregated balcony. Motels and hotels gave travelers options. Similar districts grew up at the heart of the black neighborhoods in East and North Nashville.

But the city developed a "pyramid" zoning code, which meant that land was zoned according to its perceived value. Property zoned for residential use was of higher value, and so it was protected from the incursion of commercial interests. Property zoned for commercial or industrial use could be used for single-family dwellings, but at any point, a developer could come into the middle of the neighborhood and start building anything he or she desired.

Most white neighborhoods were zoned as residential areas. African-American neighborhoods were zoned as commercial and industrial properties.

In 1949, the city administration claimed 96 acres in Hell's Half Acre. They justified it by saying they would rid the city of vice. The plat included six historic African-American churches, a business district, schools and other sites of community life. The city replaced the neighborhood with the State Library and Archives, a large office building, a six-lane parkway, terraced parking lots and green space. They announced that they would replace the rest of the neighborhood with a planned municipal auditorium and private development. Few provisions were made for the people who lost their homes.

There was "a view that Nashville had held for some time that suggested that one of the major problems with downtowns was people," former Mayor Bill Purcell explains to me as we look out the window of his high-rise downtown law office. "That if you could eliminate the people, then the city would be successful. … They banned vices; they banned activities that they felt were detrimental to civic life, and they banned residential living."

Urban redevelopment accelerated over the next several decades, and it bore down upon other black neighborhoods around the city. The 1954 Federal Housing Act offered to pay up to 90 percent of the cost if Nashville would raze unwanted buildings and replace them with superhighways. The city planners cleared the edge of East Nashville for a new interstate. They emptied another 400 acres for warehousing and industrial use. Another highway was routed through Edgehill, a lower-income, predominantly minority community. Black leaders began worrying that urban renewal would become "Negro removal."

New suburban developments popped up just outside the city's limits. The interstates proved to be effective walls between the new developments and the city's centers.

Neighborhood covenants controlled who could buy the houses, and so these areas were up to 98 percent white. Nashville grew increasingly segregated.

OPRY STAR SMELLS GOOD CHICKEN

Over the past 80 years, Thornton Prince's hot chicken business has wandered through black Nashville. The first BBQ Chicken Shack sat at the corner of Jefferson Street and 28th Avenue, near Tennessee A&I's campus and just down the street from Jefferson Street Missionary Baptist Church.

From the beginning, the restaurant was an unusual place. It was not the Princes' primary source of income. Thornton had a farm. His brothers worked for the post office or at other restaurants.

"It was just a little substitute to try to get over," Andre Jeffries tells me. "Try to get some more bills paid."

Since they had other jobs, they opened the restaurant after their workday ended and they stayed open later than any other restaurant in town: midnight during the week and until 4 a.m. on the weekends.

"That's one tradition that I try to keep, being open that late," Jeffries says. "It's grown on me. I'm a night owl now."

Because the restaurant was a late-night place, Jeffries and her siblings didn't grow up eating there.

"My father would bring it home and put it on the stove on Saturday night," she remembers. "When we'd get up on Sunday morning getting ready to go to Sunday school and then to church, I'd always see that little greasy bag on the stove. Hey, we were tackling it because he wouldn't bring more than one or two pieces, and that would make us mad."

After a few years, the Chicken Shack moved downtown into Hell's Half Acre and close to the Ryman Auditorium, home of the Grand Ole Opry in its heyday.

"When he drove to the Opry on Saturday nights, he could smell something really wonderful but couldn't figure out where it was coming from," said Lorrie Morgan, the country singer and daughter of George Morgan, a Country Music Hall of Famer who was a regular on the Opry stage from the late 1940s through the early 1970s, in the cookbook "Around the Opry Table." One night, he tracked the smell to the BBQ Chicken Shack. He loved the food and the hours. Pretty soon, the Opry stars were headed there after every performance.

Segregation complicated the restaurant's new popularity. The Princes needed a place to seat their white celebrity clientele without alienating their black customers. They constructed an ingenious compromise. They built a separate room for their white guests, but it was at the back of the building. Whites walked through the main dining room and the kitchen to reach it.

"It was quite a nice room. ... We sat out front on these benches," Jeffries says as she rubs an unpadded white booth that looks like the church pews I grew up sitting in. "I don't know how old these benches are, but I remember them when I was a child, and I'm almost 70 years old."

"Black people have never been segregated from the Caucasians," she continues. "Caucasians separated us. ... As far as segregation is concerned, that is a Caucasian problem." She claps her hands together and shakes her head. "Have mercy!"

The BBQ Chicken Shack was in the middle of the Hell's Half Acre urban renewal project. The Princes relocated. Their new space was too far from town. They moved again, choosing a block building at 17th and Charlotte, the heart of a black community north of downtown. It sat "just about where the Krystal's is," Jeffries clarifies for me.

NASHVILLE'S SIT-INS

Desegregation was a two-edged sword for many African-Americans. Racism severely limited their lives and opportunities. They had poorer school systems and fewer good job options. They were prohibited from moving into the best neighborhoods. They were denied loans and mortgages. They were expected to treat all whites with deference, even as they were mistreated. Any challenge to this system was punished with violence.

At the same time, segregation gave African-Americans even more reason to develop separate businesses and community centers. Black schools, churches and businesses became sites of resistance where the next generation learned about black heroes and black history. The BBQ Chicken Shack might not have lasted if it hadn't first been fostered within Nashville's black neighborhoods.

In 1954, the United States Supreme Court ruled that public schools had to desegregate. They could have announced a timeframe for it; instead, the justices said desegregation had to happen with "all deliberate speed."

Many communities used that wishy-washy language to push desegregation off or years or even decades. In

Nashville, a young black man named Robert Kelley walked past all-white East High School, over the Cumberland River and through downtown to all-black Pearl High School. His family filed a lawsuit in 1956, arguing the city should open East High to him. The Rev. Henry Maxwell filed a similar suit because his kids were bused from south of Nashville to the other side of the city, a 45-minute ride. To settle these cases, the courts announced that beginning in the fall of 1957, Nashville public schools would desegregate one grade per year in what became known as the "Nashville Plan."

The school board gerrymandered the school districts so that only about 100 black first-graders were eligible. Nine enrolled. White "segregation academies" and white flight further undermined efforts to integrate the schools. Seven years later, fewer than 800 black students were in formerly all-white schools. Black teachers and principals faced demotions or layoffs as the city consolidated the system.

The next stage in Nashville's civil-rights struggle happened in February 1960. A few weeks earlier, students in Greensboro, North Carolina, had sat at a downtown lunch counter and demanded service. Inspired by their example, students from Fisk, the American Baptist Theological Seminary and Tennessee A&I organized similar protests in Nashville. Black shoppers boycotted downtown businesses.

Local civil rights attorney Z. Alexander Looby headed up the team of lawyers defending the arrested students. His house was bombed in mid-April, though no one was injured. In response, several thousand protesters marched from Fisk to downtown. The mayor met them on the courthouse steps. Diane Nash, a Fisk University student who would help found the Student Nonviolent Coordinating Committee, demanded, "Mayor West, do you think it is wrong to discriminate against a person solely on the basis of their race or color?"

"Yes," he replied. He added, "That's up to the store managers, of course." The Tennessean left out his addendum in its coverage. The "Whites Only" signs came down.

Compared to many other cities, desegregation was relatively peaceful in Nashville, but this may have been because residential segregation and urban renewal had already separated the races from each other. Official, or de jure, segregation may not have seemed as necessary when interstates and building codes had ensured blacks and whites would not live, study, eat or work together.

FROM ALL OVER THE WORLD

When Thornton Prince died, his brother Will took over. His wife Maude ran the business when he passed.

Prince's first real competition happened because the family had a falling out with their cook, Bolton Polk. In the late 1970s, he left to open his own place, which he named Columbo's Chicken Shack. He served his own version of hot chicken. He added his wife's chess pies and potato salad. This launched a new debate among generations of hot-chicken devotees. Which restaurant had the better food? Which had the hotter chicken?

The first Columbo's was near Prince's in the same black neighborhood off Charlotte Avenue. Polk eventually moved his business just across the river from downtown Nashville.

That was where former Nashville Mayor Bill Purcell first encountered the dish.

"As soon as I had this hot chicken I knew it was unlike anything I'd ever had," he says to me. "It was one of the best things I ever had."

By 1980, it was time for a new generation of Princes to take over the restaurant. Andre Prince Jeffries was a recently divorced mother of two. Her parents had been helping her raise her daughters, but her mother was dying of cancer. Her parents worried that Jeffries' job in city government would not be enough for her to care for her children on her own. Great Aunt Maude decided Jeffries should take over Prince's. Her mother told her to accept the offer.

Jeffries renamed the restaurant.

"I took out the BBQ because this was never barbecue," she says. She also decided it was time to relocate. "When I took over, it seemed like every weekend we were getting robbed."

In 1989, Prince's Chicken Shack moved to its current location in East Nashville. It's in a strip mall that gentrification hasn't touched yet. On one side of it is Entrepreneur Clothing. On the day I visited, a deep bass rhythm pumped through the open door onto the street. Next to that is a customer-less Chinese restaurant and a nail salon. The parking lot is potholed, and when Prince's is busy, guests bump their way to an unpaved lot next door. The area is best known for prostitution and drug deals.

"You've got to earn the respect of the guys around here," Jeffries says, shrugging.

She talks about the memorabilia that used to be in the restaurant. Many pieces have been stolen, including photographs of her family, plaques and awards given to the restaurant, and a set of autographed plates from the celebrities who frequent Prince's. Jeffries had hoped to move the restaurant again, somewhere nicer and newer.

"We were supposed to move to 10th and Jefferson, but a lot of politics got involved," she says a little sadly. A new baseball stadium was planned for the area. "If I had it my way, we'd have a shack-type building but upscale on the interior with a big old potbellied stove in the center of it," she tells me.

"My mother always said, if you have what people want, they will make their way to your door," Jeffries says, patting the table in front of her. "You can tell, this is certainly not an upscale bird place. This is my little hole in the wall, but people have made their way here from all over the world. All over the world."

Columbo's was also trapped by the improvements happening around Nashville. In the late 1990s, Nashville won an NFL football team. The Houston Oilers became the Tennessee Titans. Columbo's sat right where the new football stadium was supposed to go. Bolton Polk closed his restaurant, and he died before he could reopen it.

THE BIG CITY, MINUS PEOPLE

The public projects accelerated in the late '60s. I-40 was built in 1968, and it cut through the heart of Jefferson Street. Because the city had zoned the region as commercial and industrial, black homeowners had few protections or ways to resist.

"We thought that we were saving the city," former Mayor Purcell explains to me. "But that wasn't going to save the city. There is no city that has been successful merely as a collection of suburban places."

"When the interstate was built, there were no exit ramps," Reavis Mitchell, a historian at Fisk University, told The Tennessean. Fifty percent of Jefferson Street's residents moved. One hundred twenty businesses closed. "All those major vital things within the inner city were blocked off. North Nashvillians were suspicious to why they were being isolated and wondered if the interstate project was in response to the marches and sit-ins."

Demolition continued into the 1970s. Developers pitched ideas to tear down more of the historic neighborhoods, replacing them with public housing, industrial warehouses and strip malls.

"I was still not sure about Nashville, and I'm not sure Nashville was sure about Nashville," Purcell says. "It was not clear what we wanted to do. ... There was a history and a practice of believing that if you did not have it here, we could go to Chicago or New York or Atlanta to buy it or see it or do it."

This was the Nashville of my childhood. Downtown was a handful of honky-tonks catering to tourists who wandered about, dazed by rhinestones, whiskey and country cover bands. Then came the lawyers' offices, banks and insurance corporations, which emptied as soon as business hours ended. Ringing all of that were strip clubs, car lots and interstates.

The first big preservation fight occurred when a plan emerged to tear down historic Second Avenue and replace it with a skyscraper. The economy was not strong enough to support the development, and the preservationists won. People started debating whether progress meant erasing or celebrating the past.

"It's all well and good to want to be the Athens of the South and to be a center of learning, but it's the city's obligation to ensure that it's so," Purcell says. "A city has to be safe, the whole city, not just parts of it or neighborhoods in it.

"By and large, this is the late '80s now, downtown Nashville was suffering from Nashville's own decision that the future of downtowns was not certain and certainly not required," he summarizes.

We're talking in the conference room of his law firm, which overlooks downtown.

"We had made periodic efforts to salvage what we had and other competitive efforts to knock down and replace what we had."

Purcell beckons me to the window. He points out the places where there was once a garbage incinerator, derelict buildings and empty lots, right in the heart of the city.

"Only about 900 people lived downtown," he says.

LORRIE AND SAMMY STRIKE OUT

Before Bolton Polk passed, he taught his nephew Bolton Matthews to make his chicken. Polk never wrote down his secrets, and his nephew has supposedly followed his example.

"He's the only one that fixes the recipe," his wife and business partner Dollye Ingram-Matthews told an interviewer with the Southern Foodways Alliance. "I can just tell you parts of it are probably made from pepper bomb spray."

Ingram-Matthews made hot fish. In 1997, they combined their secret spicy recipes and opened Bolton's Spicy Chicken and Fish in a small, low concrete block building on Main Street. It's a block from East Park, where the annual Hot Chicken Festival happens.

"I think it's popular in Nashville because there are a lot of people living today that had ancestors stuck on pepper," Dollye Ingram says. "Maybe they had hypertension and couldn't use salt, so they used pepper instead. ... A couple of generations like that, and you know you just got the clientele for hot and spicy chicken."

Then came perhaps the oddest venture in the hot-chicken story, hotchickens.com. It was started in 2001 when the Internet felt new. It wasn't a hot-chicken delivery service; it was a restaurant. And yes, .com was part of the name and even on the building's sign.

The restaurant was founded by country music stars Lorrie Morgan and Sammy Kershaw. Morgan learned to love hot chicken by eating it with her father, George. Food writer John T. Edge described hotchickens.com as "a gingham-trimmed fast-food outlet that ... reflects the peculiar Nashville geek-in-a-cowboy-hat zeitgeist." Debts from the restaurant eventually drove Kershaw into Chapter 13 bankruptcy. Their marriage ended in mutual restraining orders. Morgan tried again, underwriting Lorrie Morgan's Hot Chicken Cafe inside a gambling resort in Alabama. That effort attracted a governor's office investigation.

HOT CHICKEN AS A SYMBOL

When I came back home in 2013, Nashville was more than 10 percent larger than it had been when I left less than a decade earlier, and it's surrounded by communities that have grown by as much as 44 percent.

The tourist strip is busier and glitzier than ever. High rise condominiums have popped up among the business buildings. A new symphony center hosts concerts, speakers and community events. The Nashville Convention Center and the Music City Center draw thousands of people to town every weekend. The Bridgestone Arena seats close to 20,000 people and is home to the Nashville Predators hockey team, which has shocked their hometown and become a competitive club. Unfortunately, the same can't be said of the Titans these last few seasons.

Even more surprising to me, my friends live in East Nashville, a region of the city I remember as having a few antiquated businesses, many abandoned houses and large public housing complexes.

East Nashville's development was partially Mother Nature's fault. Tornadoes struck Nashville in April 1998. One of them swept through downtown. Another one devastated the neighborhoods of East Nashville. Three hundred homes were destroyed. A Regional/Urban Design Assistance Team formed to make suggestions for how to redevelop and rehab that quadrant of the city. They recommended creating public/private partnerships, building infrastructure tying the neighborhoods to downtown, creating design guidelines and encouraging investment.

"The two greatest treasures East Nashville offers are its diversity and authenticity," they wrote in their final report. "Throughout the nation, new 'neo-traditional' communities are being planned and developed in the hope of replicating the feeling that this community offers."

Today, East Nashville's crime rates are falling. New magnet and charter schools are commandeering the public school buildings. Some historic homes are being carefully restored. Others are being razed and replaced with new, high-priced developments. Restaurants and coffee shops and boutique clothing stores form the heart of new, trendy business districts catering to a hipster crowd.

The improvements are billed as helping the entire community, but they are coming at a cost to the people who have lived there for generations. Many of them are getting priced out of their homes. Some of the black residents whose ancestors first settled East Nashville are being forced into the suburbs where whites used to live. Others are ending up in overcrowded, low-income pockets of the city.

In this era of change and loss, residents and visitors alike are anxious to celebrate what is historic about the town. Hot chicken has become shorthand for the area's various traditions, a de rigueur part of being from here.

THEY COME BACK TO THE REAL THING

Hot chicken has left the neighborhood. But new restaurants specializing in the dish are popping up across town.

"They're like pizza places, all over," Andre Jeffries tells me. "Everywhere you look, there's a new one opening."

The craze for hot chicken started in 2007 with the first Hot Chicken Festival. Mayor Purcell was stepping down after two terms. He still went to Prince's regularly, referring to it as his second office. He urged his friends and colleagues to try hot chicken, though when he brought new customers to the restaurant, he would pull Jeffries aside. "He'll tell us to give it to them hot, don't give it to them mild. You don't know if he's their worst enemy or what!"

Purcell also set Prince's up with free advertising, making them the face of the new hot-chicken trend. "Why?" Jeffries asks. "Because he knows I have to pay my bills."

Purcell was looking for a way to celebrate the city, which was approaching its bicentennial.

"Hot chicken is truly our indigenous food," he explains. "It seemed a way to convene the city around something special to us, worth celebrating but also allowed everybody to participate."

He founded a festival committee, and they decided to put the festivities in East Park, which is near the entrance to East Nashville. This meant it was close to downtown, but it wouldn't be swallowed up by other events happening in the city.

"And I was the mayor," Purcell adds, with a little smirk. "East Park was close to where I live."

The festival quickly grew in popularity, introducing people to the dish. Hot-chicken cooking contests became part of events around the city. New hot-chicken restaurants were founded, most of them run by young white men in popular gentrifying districts.

Isaac Beard was the first of the new generation of hot-chicken restaurateurs. He opened Pepperfire Chicken in 2010.

"I believe I was born to do something with hot chicken," he told food columnists Jane and Michael Stern. "I am a hot-chicken evangelist."

The most successful of these new ventures is Hattie B's, owned by Nick Bishop Jr. and his dad Nick Sr. The first Hattie B's opened in 2012 in Midtown, right in the heart of a new, hip area.

"Hattie B's is almost in both Music Row (the area where country recording studios are located) and the campuses of both Vanderbilt and Belmont Universities, making it a much nicer area than Prince's seedy strip mall," food blogger Dan Angell wrote of his visit there. "The idea of being in a more protected area was appealing to us, and since you can't go through Nashville without having experienced hot chicken, Hattie B's was the choice." Soon, the Midtown location had a loyal following. They opened a new spot on the edge of a rapidly gentrifying neighborhood once known as the Nations, which developers are trying to force us to rename Historic West Town.

I asked Andre Prince Jeffries if she's worried about losing her customers.

"My customers, they try all these different places that are popping up," she says. "They come right back here. Might take 'em a little while, but they come back to the real thing. They tell me all the time, 'You still got it.' 'Course that makes me feel good. Have mercy." Her only question, she insists, is which family member will take the restaurant next.

THE STRANGER TO TRADITION EATS HOT CHICKEN

Yes, I have now eaten hot chicken. I decided to start with the original, so I got a leg of Prince's the day I interviewed Andre Jeffries.

It was getting late, so I took my food to go like most of the other customers. By the time I placed my order, someone else was sitting in my booth. I stood along the wall, waiting for my food and balancing my recorder bag on my feet. A B-grade horror flick played on a flat-screen TV suspended on the wall across from me. I watched a plastic dinosaur chase stranded castaways down a beach.

Jeffries saw me standing there. I heard an argument start up in the back. She told them to rush my order. "But she just got here!" a woman said. "No, she's been here for over an hour," Jeffries replied. A young man came out with my sack of food a few minutes later.

There are people who order their chicken so hot that Jeffries sends them home to eat it in private. There are people who go with chicken one notch down. They sometimes ask for wet paper towels to lay over their eyes. Food reviewers warn hot-chicken newbies to wash their hands before using the restroom or touching any other sensitive body parts.

If you want to read the graphic details of what absurdly hot poultry can do to a person, what happens to your body when you eat food so spicy that you shouldn't be seen in public, well, I'm a wimp. I grew up in a household where adding garlic made a dish spicy. I ordered my chicken mild. I added a side of coleslaw, figuring I could use it to cut the heat.

It was very good fried chicken, moist and crispy at the same time, but it was warmer than I like my food. While I'd love to talk more with Andre Jeffries, I'm not sure I'll ever be the hot-chicken devotee so many Nashvillians have become.

CULTURAL TOUCHSTONES VS. HIPSTER TRENDS

One day in graduate school, I went to a meeting at the Center for the Study of the American South. The speaker had spent the past year photographing the U.S./Mexico border, recording the terror and danger faced by undocumented workers who fled their homelands for the opportunities the United States represented.

It was the spring of 2008, and North Carolina was in the throes of an immigration debate and newly awakened by the pending nomination of Barack Obama. Issues of race and equality were on our minds, but we were also historians. We could all riff on the discouraging realitiesof modern America, like the fact that public schools were more segregated than they had been at any time since 1965 and income inequality was growing. Our conversation grew increasingly cynical.

Then William Ferris chimed in. Ferris is a noted folklorist whose wife is a prominent foodways scholar. He is one of those public intellectuals whose lists of achievements should make him terrifying, but he has a deeply kind streak that makes him a student favorite.

Ferris said that the popularity of Mexican culture encouraged him. He pointed out that Mexican restaurants are growing ubiquitous, and in each establishment, customers met people affected by the immigration debate. Maybe restaurant-goers would get to know their servers, fall in love with their food, dance to the music they heard playing over the sound systems and thus learn to empathize with immigrants.

At the time, I vehemently disagreed with him. It was the only time I dared to do so. I used the African-American experience as my example. "Whites have eaten fried chicken for centuries now," I remember saying. "Segregation still exists."

But these days, I find myself hoping he was right. Is the hot-chicken craze helping Nashville create a new history? Or is hot chicken being stripped of its cultural meaning as it's moved out of the neighborhood? Can a simple chicken dish be trusted with healing the divisions that have taken generations to form? Or will it become nothing more than Nashville's newest hipster trend?

EATIN' THAT RAINBOW STEW

The 9th Annual Music City Hot Chicken Festival happened on July 4, 2015. It was an unusual Independence Day for Tennessee, with a high of only 82 and an almost guaranteed chance of rain. Diehard hot-chicken lovers still braved the weather, ducking under golf umbrellas or into the beer tents when rain started falling.

I showed up for the mid-morning parade that kicks off the day's official events. I was supposed to be meeting a guy for a first date. I was counting on Andre Prince Jeffries' theory, that this chicken would give us something to talk about. But as I got out of my car, I got a text from him saying he would be late. Then I realized I had forgotten my umbrella. It seemed an inauspicious beginning to the both relationship and the day.

I found a seat on a low concrete wall along the parade route and started making notes about the folks around me. Though the crowd's racial demographics didn't match East

Nashville's neighborhoods or even the numbers in Nashville generally, it was the closest thing to a mixed gathering I've seen in Nashville (outside of a sporting event).

But very few individuals mingled with anyone other than the people they came with. I wondered if that was partly because the weather kept numbers low. Groups could sit comfortably distanced from everyone else.

The parade was what Momma would call "homegrown." Two police on motorcycles led it followed by a small brass band. The rest of the parade was made up of: four antique firetrucks which judiciously chirped their sirens, trying to show off for the crowd without scaring the babies; a series of municipal candidates and their supporters who hurled candy at bystanders; a couple of local businesses with people tossing beads out the door of their company vehicles; one home-converted topless wood-paneled station wagon labelled #TheDoose that carried a handful of very cool looking 20-somethings; and three tatted-up members of the Nashville Rollergirls, who whipped in and out of the other groups.

After the parade, I walked back through East Park to the main stage, where the Shelby Bottom String Band was entertaining the crowd, filling time until Bill Purcell stepped on stage to say a few words.

"We're going to play Bill's favorite," the lead singer told the crowd. They started in on a Merle Haggard classic:

Eating rainbow stew with a silver spoon
Underneath that sky of blue
We'll all be drinking that free bubble-up
And eating that rainbow stew

Purcell wasn't ready when they were finished the song, so they soldiered on through another couple of numbers.

My guy showed up about the same time Purcell did. We wandered around, looking into our various options. Lines had started forming in front of each of the hot-chicken tents. He told me he lived down the road from the new Hattie B's in the Nations and ate there all the time. I told him the story of Prince's founding.

The line for Prince's stretched the length of the green, past the lines for Hattie B's and Pepperfire and Bolton's. At the end of the green, the queue took a sharp turn, wrapping around Prince's competitors.

A curious thing was happening. Folks at the back of the Prince's line stayed in their groups, chatting with the people they came with. But by the time they reached the bend in the queue, they were running out of things to say to their friends. They stood, arms crossed and hips cocked, staring into space.

But after a few more minutes of waiting, they started talking to the others in line around them, telling strangers the story of when they first tried hot chicken and trading insider knowledge of what to order from the other hot chicken joints.

— *Rachel L. Martin is a Nashville-based writer whose essays have also been published In The Atlantic, CityLab, Narratively, and elsewhere.*

First Published December 17, 2013

Wild Miles on the Big River

•••

BOYCE UPHOLT

The Mississippi River is big, dangerous and industrialized. But from St. Louis down to the Louisiana bayous, more than 500 miles of the great American river remain wild. And you could have no better guide through the river's ever-decreasing "wild miles" than John Ruskey.

From five miles upstream the boys spied the electrical lines, arcing over the river and buttressed by t wo sets of truss towers. But why would they care? The Mississippi River is wide. What are the chances you'd hit a little pylon?

Then they were 100 yards away, caught in fast water. They paddled hard, but their raft — ungainly, hand-built, their home for five months now — would not budge from its path. As it slammed against concrete, both boys fell. Supplies scattered, journals and a guitar and precious food disappearing into February water flowing cold and fast. The front of the raft began to ride up the pillar; the back slipped into the river. Then, snapping like a cracker, the raft came apart. Both boys plunged in.

One of those boys, John Ruskey, had always been drawn to water. There's a story his family tells: At age 2, young John often stared out the window at the pond on the far side of his Colorado road. One day, unaccompanied and unannounced, he walked out the door, seeking the pond. As a first grader, his peers called him the Weatherman; a teacher phoned home because during a downpour he refused to come inside. When he graduated from prep school in 1982, Ruskey ventured to the Mississippi River.

He and a friend camped in Wisconsin, building a 12-by-24 foot raft from refuse and scrap wood. They floated south through winter, warming themselves alongside a fire built in a halved oil drum. They sipped coffee and played chess with pieces they'd carved from willow branches and watched America slip by.

Just past Memphis — one of the most memorable sights on the southern Mississippi according to Ruskey, shimmering on its bluff above the water — they noted and ignored the electrical lines. They resumed a game of chess.

Ruskey cannot piece together all that happened. He knows he went numb, and that he and his friend lashed together the pieces of wreckage they could grab. They heaved their chests out of the frigid water. As the sun slipped down, Ruskey was shivering, nearly catatonic, ready to let go of life. Given the cold water and their lack of precautions (Ruskey was not wearing neoprene, as he does now on cold days), he probably should have died.

He has written an account of the wreck. It serves as a kind of creation myth, an explanation of the man Ruskey has become. He describes his delirious exit from the industrial outskirts of Memphis and his arrival in a realm unimpaired by the toils of mankind. The boys washed up on Cat Island, just past the Mississippi border, where a flock of red-winged blackbirds was settling into the darkening woods.

He made a promise, to himself and to the river: If he survived the night, he would return to this beautiful place.

THE RIVERGATOR

Thirty-three years later, John Ruskey is a quiet man. If you meet him in the street, he can seem removed, even standoffish; an interlocutor struggles to find the right questions to ask. He's self-possessed, so much so that he seems bored, or maybe bewildered, by our workaday world.

Once, years after that crash, he found himself working an office job. Every afternoon he would get overwhelmed and claustrophobic, he's said. "I had to get out," he once told an interviewer. "I had to go."

He would go to the Mississippi River.

If you see Ruskey there, on his river, you see a man come alive. His eyes sharpen. His posture loosens. He sings as he paddles. Every sight inspires a story — an abandoned house on stilts recalls an anecdote from Twain; the fog atop the river reminds of him being lost on the river at night. He shares his wisdom: ornithology, astronomy, physics, geology, navigation, more.

I've seen him perch in a drowned willow, floating down the river. When it came alongside his canoe, he scrambled out onto the limbs to investigate what detritus had been caught. Then, grinning, he rode the tree a half mile downstream.

Here, on the river that almost killed him, Ruskey found peace — and a career. He has almost certainly spent more hours paddling the Mississippi than anyone else alive. He leads custom river tours. He rents canoes and kayaks. He mentors low-income students, teaching them to build canoes and camp and serve as river guides. He paints watercolor interpretations of the river, which he hands out on his journeys as a way to introduce wary locals to the wilderness that flows through their backyard.

It took him years to get back to the river: wandering years. "I was just a kid off the street," Ruskey told me. "I had a backpack and a guitar." He returned to Mississippi not to see the river but to learn the blues. For a while, that music sent him touring the world. But he would always come back to Mississippi, where that river ran relentlessly south. He could never stay away long.

Now he's nearly completed what might be considered his life's great work. "Rivergator," it's called, a document that when finished will be more than 1,000 pages long. It contains plenty of history, some lovely storytelling and lots of philosophical wisdom. But really it is a guide: Mile by mile, it leads readers down the Lower Mississippi River Water Trail, which, stretching from St. Louis to the Gulf of Mexico, will be the longest river-based water trail in the United States.

Somehow, he's got to convince a nation that their beliefs about their iconic river are all wrong: that it's not dirty, not dangerous — at least not too dangerous. That it's exactly the place you want to be. First, though, he's got to get to the water.

FLOOD STAGE & RISING

Ruskey naps, tucked between coolers and luggage in the trunk of an old Chevy Suburban. The truck barrels south through Mississippi darkness; a 33-foot wooden canoe, built by Ruskey, is strapped to a trailer behind us. It's March 2015, one of those hazy hours before dawn. Somewhere before Vicksburg, Ruskey sits up. In Natchez, he pulls out his cell phone. This might be the best office space he'll have for a week.

Ruskey woke today at 1 a.m. to load the canoe; for a week straight he's been up each day before dawn, seeking a few quiet hours to work. A voyage like this requires a flurry of emails. He must consult maps and weather forecasts and compare the river levels at more than 20 gauges to predict its speed and how quickly it's rising. It's high enough right now that, according to the warnings Ruskey has included in "Rivergator," paddlers should not be out.

Creeks and bogues slip past outside the truck windows, thin lines of water trickling into the woods. This is how Americans know their rivers, Ruskey often says. Even the famous Mississippi is, for most of us, just a glimmer of water through a guardrail as our car speeds over a bridge. Where Ruskey lives, in the Mississippi Delta, the big river is hidden behind levees, so that even those who live within a stone's throw must make an effort to reach the water. That's the way most want it, thanks to memories and legends from 100 years of devastating floods. (The most recent, in 2011, caused several billion dollars in damage). The ports of New Orleans and Memphis, where the river is most visible, stink of oil and fish. Many believe that the river is just a sewer for toxic waste.

Ruskey disagrees. He considers nearly two-thirds of the riverbank along this southern stretch of the Mississippi wild. Indeed, in this part of the Deep South, it is some of the only wilderness left.

Few see it. While more than 600 people summited Mount Everest last year and more than 700 through-hiked the Appalachian Trail, Ruskey believes only 50 paddled the length of the river.

In 1998, 16 years after the Coast Guard rescued him off Cat Island, Ruskey incorporated the Quapaw Canoe Company. Based in Clarksdale, Mississippi, it was the first wilderness outfitter along the Lower Mississippi. In 2011 he began compiling Rivergator. For four years, he's led expeditions down a hundred miles of river at a time, ensuring the details are up to date. More than 900 miles of guidance are already available online; the project will be completed in late 2016. It is, Ruskey says, the culmination of more than 30 years of work.

Today begins the penultimate Rivergator expedition. Since the final journey will be down "Cancer Alley," lined by heavy industry from Baton Rouge to the coast, this is Ruskey's last voyage through his beloved "wild miles."

But now, all his careful plans have gone awry. In Woodville, where the crew gathers at a gas-station café to fuel up on soul food and collect its final few members, Ruskey learns that the flooding has washed out the road to the boat ramp. It's the only river access for miles.

"THAT YOUR IDEA OF A GOOD TIME?"

There are eight of us: two journalists, two paying customers, a hired videographer, plus Ruskey and two trusted guides. Mark Peoples, who played pro football for the New York Giants, encountered Ruskey during one of his daily visits to the riverside in St. Louis, his hometown. Seeking a way to serve the river, Peoples was inspired by Ruskey's passion. After a trial expedition with Quapaw, he moved to Clarksdale — into an old bar that sits above Ruskey's office — and became a guide. Now everyone knows him as River. Braxton Braden, known as Brax, is retired after 20 years in the Navy. They call Ruskey John or Johnny or Driftwood Johnny.

Of this crew, I have the least experience on the big river: none at all. I've arranged to join the trip for its first three days. While everyone cinches shut dry-bags and tugs on boots and wetsuits, I watch to see how it's done. The truck is backed up on a farm road that, a few feet beyond us, has been seized by the flood.

Such is the nature of rivers. They are not the stable, identifiable places to which we're accustomed in the age of Google Maps. Change the zoom on Google's satellite map, in fact, and you'll see the river change. Different photos show different water levels, which vary up to 30 feet in a typical year. Dry land turns to back-channels; islands emerge from the water. Now this pasture has joined with the river system.

"We're getting onto the biggest river in North America," Ruskey says later, "and the only access in southern Mississippi is through a cow ditch."

A snake skims across the surface of the ditch. Ruskey dives in, baptizing himself in scummy water.

We've been sent here by the mayor of Woodville, who heard that Ruskey was in town. He arrived at the café with a delegation of locals, who unfurled a surveyor's map and pointed out a route: Paddle a few miles across this flooded field to the Buffalo River, then a few miles more to the Mississippi. Just one problem. This is private land. A phone call has assured our safe passage; down some of these dirt roads, Ruskey says, the locals aren't too friendly.

We met our one-woman welcoming committee in Fort Adams, which, when New Orleans was foreign property, was the U.S. port of entry on the river. Now there's little more than a one-room store that sells fishing supplies. Our contact, a middle-aged woman whose family farms nearby, stands in the dirt lot and squints at the canoe.

"That your idea of a good time?"

Though the sun is past its zenith, Ruskey does not rush. He chats with the locals, as he chats with everyone he meets, waging a slow campaign of hearts and minds. He gives a copy of the latest Rivergator poster, a reproduction of a watercolor map, to the storekeeper. An earlier edition is already tacked to a wall inside.

The Lower Mississippi is a big river, fed by the collected waters of many tributaries — the Missouri, the Ohio, its own headwaters in the Minnesota lakes. You could call it the real Mississippi, the place where the waters of the continent finally merge. The river basin drains portions of 31 states, from New York to Montana, over 40 percent of the continental U.S.

Controlling that water requires infrastructure. The woman at the store is fluent in its technical terms, and talks of spillways and the distribution of flow. She has clear opinions, too: The water floods here and not downstream, she says, because Louisiana farmers have more money and power. The U.S. government, which controls the river, cannot possibly keep everyone happy.

Another woman pulls into the lot, seeking gas at the empty pumps, and our host discloses the nature of our strange quest. River chats with this new arrival. As we drive away, he shares her story: She lost a son to the Mississippi. Fishing without a life jacket, he fell in, and was drowned by the weight of the water that rushed inside his boots.

Now, after a brief ceremony, we paddle out. What is usually a hunting club is hidden beneath five feet of flat backwater. Birds of prey sit watchful in the treetops; colonies of fire ants have linked their legs to form a fabric that floats on the water and shimmers as they move their legs. The natural world thrives in this flood.

AN UGLY BIT OF RIVER

As we arrive on the water of the Mississippi, I hear an incessant ringing tone. It comes from the control structures, massive metal floodgates built nearby to constrain the river to its path. It's a warning: Stay away. On the maps Ruskey carries, a note declares the structure's inflow channels "very dangerous... Under no circumstances should any vessel attempt to enter."

"If you paddled into that, you'd have to make some quick decisions," Ruskey says.

He estimates that more lives have been lost on the

Mississippi and its tributaries than on every other North American river combined. We stay on the river's far side; I see the structure only when we stop and climb the bluff.

Despite the dangers, in Ruskey's care I feel safe. He is gentle on the river, and amid close quarters and novice expeditioners he never shows any sign of frustration. Our first full day begins with a prayerful speech; Ruskey compares our crew to a flock of birds. The more that watch the river, he says, the safer it will be.

After the speech, Ruskey performs the same ritual that launches all his trips, a smudge ceremony he learned from a Cherokee healer. While River beats a hand drum, Ruskey waves a smoking bundle of sage over the canoe and its passengers, who turn to face each direction. The ceremony is meant to help us transition from our lives on land to our lives on water.

"We did that in honor of the Mother Mississippi," he says when the ceremony is through. "It makes me a little bit sad to be leaving the big river."

Most of this expedition will not be on the Mississippi; it will follow the Atchafalaya River to the Gulf. Thirty percent of the Mississippi's water is diverted down this distributary, a rate that is set by law. In 1950, as engineers worried that the Atchafalaya might seize the entirety of the bigger river, Congress declared that "the distribution of flow and sediment in the Mississippi and Atchafalaya Rivers is now in desirable proportions and should be so maintained." (Thus the control structures and their warnings.)

Such seizures are the nature of rivers, when left alone. A river carries soil, which it deposits as it slows, building up new land. Gradually its path to its mouth grows longer. The

Atchafalaya now offers a shorter and faster route to the Gulf — making it the route the water would have chosen if left to its own devices. Until the engineers arrived, the river granted itself such shortcuts roughly once every thousand years.

Ruskey is including the Atchafalaya in Rivergator because he believes that for paddlers, too, it is preferable route. South of the fork, the Mississippi is clogged with industry; the Atchafalaya is all cypress woods and back-channels. Wild miles.

Ruskey coined that phrase to describe the places on the river where there is still little evidence of the permanent intervention of mankind. The batture, or the untended land between the levees that still gets flooded each year, is a critical habitat for many species. Two-thirds of the nation's migrating birds use the Mississippi as a flyway.

Ruskey compares these riverbanks to "long landscapes," which the Pulitzer Prize-winning biologist E.O. Wilson considers key to conserving biodiversity in a world where species are gravely threatened by the actions of mankind. Long landscapes cut continent-long wilderness corridors through our developed land, allowing animals to migrate — or flee disasters. People used to say that when the South was wooded, a squirrel could travel from Arkansas to Virginia without ever touching the ground. Such long-distance travel may still be possible up and down the Mississippi, Ruskey told me, though only in a stretch five miles wide.

On the river between St. Louis and Baton Rouge, roughly 600 wild miles remain, though the number is always falling. On our first day, Ruskey pointed out a mansion perched above the Mississippi. Less than three years old, the house now disqualifies this stretch as wild.

House or no, it is not a particularly beautiful stretch of river. Sometimes that is the fault of humans, who in places have shoveled refrigerators and other large-scale waste down the riverbank — out of sight, out of mind. (Ruskey notes the coordinates of such dumping sites, as well as illegally gated back-channels, and sends them to a volunteer who works with the Waterkeeper Alliance.) But it's also one of the last days of winter, and the landscape is grim. The muddy water swells up the levee; in places, only the barren top branches are visible, grasping up from beneath the water.

YANKING OUT YOUR HEART

Three weeks later, back in Clarksdale, Ruskey and I sit in his basement office. I ask about his definition of wilderness. His answer is not at all about beauty.

"When you walk through a city park, it's pretty," he says. "You hear birds. But when you walk across a sandbar in the Mississippi, you're dwarfed by the scale of things. For me it's a humbling experience, a painful experience. Sometimes it's a frightening experience."

Ruskey says the secret to our species' success has been our ability to manipulate our environment and make it hospitable.

"But we've forgotten that it's important not to be in control." He wrote about this in his account of the raft wreck: When we let ourselves go, he says, we open ourselves to all the possibilities of the universe.

Up on the streets of Clarksdale, the Juke Joint Festival, one of the region's best-known celebrations of the blues, its native music, is in full swing. Ruskey has set up a dugout canoe demonstration so that tourists can whack at the wood with an adze. Outside his shop, advocates from a partner nonprofit ask passersby to pledge themselves as "river citizens." Out back, behind the office, tourists camp along the Sunflower River, paying $25 each to the canoe company for their spots.

Ruskey calls this office the Cave. In 1991, he moved in, just a broke kid looking to learn the blues. It was a storage space for the bar upstairs; he found a pingpong table to serve as a bed.

He was tutored for two years by the late Johnnie Billington, and later, backing James "Super Chikan" Johnson, he toured the country and played a few international gigs. He found a job as the curator at the Delta Blues Museum — a dream job, but a desk job all the same. The river became his solace.

He tells me now that the river always reminds him how he is a tiny fraction of a bigger world.

"That's very good for the ego, to get deflated," he says. "It's the purest form of reality check."

In 1996, a German tourist heard that Ruskey knew the river, and hired him as a guide. Two years later, the Quapaw Canoe Company was incorporated. (The name means "downstream people," and honors a tribe that, rather than paddle the river up to the Great Plains, followed the water south.) Over the years Ruskey has led groups for Outside Magazine, ESPNOutdoors and National Geographic, and last year appeared on "Parts Unknown," Anthony Bourdain's new travel show. Despite locals' wariness of the river, in 2013 Quapaw was named Coahoma County's business of the year. Over his years as a businessman, Ruskey settled into a more typically adult life: He married, fathered a daughter, and moved out of the Cave and into a former boarding house in town.

Now the Cave is cluttered with river driftwood, maps and stacks of magazines. Floor-to-ceiling shelves bulge with books about bluesmen and explorers. Ruskey is in his last year of payments for the building, which he bought in the early 2000s. After serving as landlord for a series of short-lived bars, Ruskey expanded the canoe company to fill all 18,000 square feet. A former distribution center for automotive parts, it now houses living quarters and hostel space, boat storage, and workshops in which Ruskey and his students carve canoes.

Last February the state demanded more than $42,000 in back taxes from the company. Ruskey had been operating under the assumption that, per federal law, activities he conducted on navigable rivers are tax-free.

"I'm not sure we'll survive this fight," he told a journalist at the time. But supporters voiced their concerns; the company delivered over a thousand pages of documentation and testimonials about their work. As a result, the state updated its tax code and abated the assessment.

As his business grew, Ruskey has invested in Clarksdale. He launched Friends of the Sunflower River, which is devoted to caring for what Ruskey calls the "blues river," since it winds past so many musical landmarks in Clarksdale and beyond. In 2011, he incorporated the Lower Mississippi River Foundation, a nonprofit that oversees his community work. Much of that work, including Rivergator, is funded by the Walton Family Foundation.

Ruskey's biggest project — more important even than Rivergator, in his eyes — is the Mighty Quapaw Apprentice Program. Johnnie Billington, his blues mentor, decomposed the music into its constituent skills and taught them one by one to local children. Ruskey applies the same logic to his various river arts.

"If you don't share what you have with the youth around you, then it's going to die when you die," he says. "I've done so much work pushing this boulder up the mountain, and I don't want it to go tumbling back down."

He did not plan to apprentice students, he says, but local youth began to hang around as he carved canoes. Someone brave would sidle up and ask what Ruskey was doing. He would answer, and then the boy would fall back into the group. Then someone else would step forward to ask if he could try. Ruskey tells me he sees something of himself in these young men.

"They're the circles that don't fit through the squares," he says.

Some have worked with Ruskey for over a decade, and now, he says, they are among the best paddlers on the river. Most are young black men. The river offers both economic and spiritual solutions in a place where options can be slim: Clarksdale, which like the surrounding Delta is majority African-American, is the seat of one of the poorest counties in America.

"We're barely scratching the surface," Ruskey says. "I just don't have the time to do it. I'd like to do a better job."

A few apprentices have decided to make careers as river guides. As Ruskey talks, his pride in these young men is apparent. But others, he tells me, come and go. They haven't found what Ruskey and Brax and River all know: that the wilderness can yank out your heart and then return you to your place in the natural order.

DON'T YOU KNOW YOU'RE CRAZY?

At the boat ramp in Louisiana where I disembark from the trip, two women in a car gawk as we come ashore.

"Don't you know you're crazy?" one says. They, too, have lost family to the water. Earlier, as we paddled the canal that would link us to the Atchafalaya, two boys fishing from a motorboat asked our destination. When they heard we were headed for the coast, one declared us insane. We were wearing life jackets; they were not.

But towboats present the paddler's greatest danger. The Mississippi is a towboat highway: The U.S. Army Corps of Engineers maintains a shipping channel at least 300 feet wide and nine feet deep, the main corridor of an inland waterway that transports more than $100 billion in goods each year. To pass between the Atchafalaya and the Mississippi, boats must use a lock, a kind of river elevator that seals at both ends so that water can be pumped in or out, raising or lowering a boat. The Mississippi, pushed up by its levees, now sits as much as 33 feet higher than the Atchafalaya at the lock.

The lockmaster is required to pass all vessels through, no matter their size. But as we approach, a truck comes screaming down the levee, honking its horn.

"We've got a visitor," River says. As a louder warning bellows from the lock, the driver spills from his truck, furiously waving his arms. I worry the metal gates will open and a towboat will plow forward into our water.

It turns out the lockmaster is simply surprised. He has never seen a boat like ours. After a few minutes of conversation, during which Ruskey hands over another of his maps, we paddle into the canyon of concrete and steel. For 15 minutes we sit while the pumps squeal and squeak and the water falls.

Biologist Paul Hartfield, a friend of Ruskey's, calls the Mississippi one of the most controlled rivers on the planet. Its floodplain, which once spread as much as 50 miles in each direction, has been reduced to just 10 percent of its historical size. One could argue that nothing on this river is wild, since its boundaries are dictated by the placement of manmade levees. Ruskey's "wild miles" are simply the places where human influence is least apparent.

When I interviewed Ruskey in the Cave, I pressed him on this fact. He pointed out that at this point human beings have altered every corner of the earth.

"Even in Antarctica carbon dioxide from vehicles is being captured by ice," he said. And in an engineered world, he added, there is something special about water: It takes away your feeling of control.

Hartfield told me his measure for wildness is whether an ecosystem remains intact. By this metric, despite the engineering, the river is quite wild. No species of fish has gone extinct on the Lower Mississippi, and over the past decade, as the Corps has emphasized the use of "notched dikes," more water has flowed into back-channels, expanding critical habitats. Pallid sturgeon populations are booming; the fat pocketbook mussel, once found only in an Arkansas tributary, has now migrated into the Mississippi. The population of the interior least tern, an endangered bird species, has, thanks to the development of new sandbars, climbed from 2,000 to 20,000.

Ruskey would love to see this wilderness expand. He told me that if we pulled back the levees and widened the floodplain, it would benefit the entire continent: Lakes would regenerate; landmass would accumulate in Louisiana; the Gulf's dead zone would shrink. It would help city folk, too: Flood control in New Orleans would be simplified.

THE WILDERNESS WITHIN

John Ruskey holds to a riverman's rule: Always stop at the first good-looking campsite.

The first night, as we paddle up to Shreve's Bar, a warm breeze blows off the island, relieving in the afternoon chill. The water is cold — 42 degrees, we estimate — but every day Ruskey is on the river, he takes a swim. At that night's driftwood campfire, Brax and River tell a story of a frozen expedition. It was December; the air temperature never rose above 32 degrees. But, in grant applications, they had promised to make this trip; they were locked in.

We are just across the river from Angola, the Louisiana penitentiary that is the country's largest maximum-security prison. A soft glow from its lights is just visible above the trees. But camped on a sandy island beach, my tent backed by a forest of willows, looking up at a sky of bright stars, I cannot imagine a more wonderfully inaccessible place.

As a boy in Colorado, Ruskey and his family packed into a van and drove into the vast Rocky Mountain wilds.

Those childhood trips instilled a democratic wilderness ethic in Ruskey: The wildest lands should be available to everyone, he thinks, and not held by private, high-priced hunting clubs, as is often the case in the South. In our interview, he told me that the Mississippi floodplain is just as wild a place as more iconic wilderness parks in the American West, though it's rarely recognized as such. Too few people have been here.

The second night we park the canoe in a tiny runnel, which by morning has become a full backwater creek. Such seasonal streams are key to river biology, providing a water source for mammals and a place for frogs to lay eggs, which in turn are consumed by fish preparing for spawn.

Ruskey sits above the creek, annotating a map. He flags potential campsites and notes a mismarked boat ramp, which, if it ever existed, is now gone. His laptop sits nearby, plugged into a portable battery, so that updates from the expedition can be posted online. Ruskey loves and hates the Internet. Now everywhere is an office, even a riverside bluff.

Each morning the world is wrapped in fog. On Shreve's Bar, we can hear the towboats churning downriver — invisible, though only a hundred yards away. A pelican loops in the sky, and we are not sure if he can see us through the clouds. While we wait for the fog to lift, the crew journals and draws and drinks river-water coffee. Ruskey disappears.

Ruskey often speaks of "finding the wilderness within," meaning the biodiversity that is still protected by the river that snakes through our developed South. But I think he is also speaking of the wilderness inside ourselves.

Hartfield told me that he has been on trips where, as soon as camp is set, Ruskey is gone. It can unnerve tourists, Hartfield thinks, to suddenly find themselves alone on the banks. Ruskey, despite a career as a tour guide, is an obvious introvert. He needs time to himself, alone in the wilderness within. Perhaps we all do.

When he is back, Ruskey sits facing the water and plays slide blues on an acoustic guitar. It is less a performance than a meditation.

As he sits on a driftwood log — and later, as he stands in the stern of the canoe, peering into the woods we pass — I feel a bit embarrassed. I've spent years trying to fit myself into the clean delineations of modern American success: paychecks and publications and grad school. But here is someone who has learned precisely what he wants and needs from life. He makes me want to devote myself to something just as deeply as he does — to words, maybe, or telling stories; to a river, to conservation, to a job, to a marriage, to goddamn anything. He makes me want to stop wasting time. No more mucking around with the strictures and niceties and control structures of society.

GONE, LIKE THE WATER

Rivergator is named for "The Navigator," a bestseller first published in 1801 and reprinted 12 times, a book that guided pioneers through the Mississippi Valley. There's irony to the name, I think: Those pioneers launched a process that's proved irreversible, and now we have the sprawling towns and highways of today's unwild South.

When we talk in the Cave, I ask Ruskey if he struggles with the idea that he is inviting more people into a place he cherishes for its emptiness. Mount Everest, to which he has compared the river, has now become dangerously congested.

"Any place can get overused," he says. "I don't know how I'd feel if I arrived on an island and there were 10 camps and 500 people. But if we don't have more people engaging with [the Mississippi River] for its natural qualities, it will eventually become more and more industrialized. We'll completely lose what wilderness we have."

When I ask how he measures his impact, his answer is simple: people. The number of apprentices who have gone through the Mighty Quapaw program. The number who stick with it. The number of river guides he has helped open partner companies or Quapaw outposts in other towns.

"There are hundreds of people up and down the river," he says.

As we talk, a man knocks on the window and waves goodbye. It's a friend, Ruskey says, who first came out on the river five or six years ago. He read about Ruskey's trips and became obsessed. His wife told him to get it out of his system and go. That backfired: Now he organizes a yearly trip.

Ruskey invites me to camp out behind the Cave that night. There are bright streetlights and roaring pickups all night, and I wake to the sound of the last festival revelers departing the nearby bar. But at dawn I'm gratified, unzipping my tent to the sight of the little Sunflower River trickling past.

That afternoon, I join a group of tourists on a day trip — three canoes and many novice paddlers. A group of women sings rounds they composed as children at summer camp. A ponytailed man holds a bongo, and while everyone else paddles, he keeps an unsteady beat. Ruskey, through it all, stays gentle. He explains the passing landscape, and when two towboats appear, he calmly guides the flotilla to safer waters.

We stop on a sandbar for lunch. Once the food is served, Ruskey is gone.

I step away from the crowd — I need a quiet moment, too — and see him. He is taking his river swim. Here, 50 miles from the beautiful island where he nearly died, Ruskey is still at home. I watch his back for the half-second it is visible, and then he is gone beneath the muddy water.

— Boyce Upholt is an award-winning Mississippi Delta-based freelance writer with a particular interest in the way we shape place and the way places shape us.

First Published January 14, 2014

A Reconciliation In Georgia

•••

JIM AUCHMUTEY

Earlier this year, Atlanta author Jim Auchmutey published "The Class of '65," a stunning book about a tortured civil-rights era triangle in Americus, Georgia: black students integrating a public school, one young white man who stood with them, and the white students who abused them all, After the book came out in April, Jim and that now older man, Greg Wittkamper, went back to Americus, where they learned even more about the power of reconciliation — and just how hard it is to achieve.

One summer a few years ago, my wife and I were on vacation at Rocky Mountain National Park when I did something that suggested I probably needed a longer vacation. There we were, surrounded by some of the greatest scenery on the continent, and I felt a twitch to check my voice mail back at the office, at The Atlanta Journal-Constitution, where I had worked as a reporter for almost 30 years.

There was a message from a former editor of mine, Ann Morris. She had gotten together with some friends from her hometown of Roanoke, Virginia, and had heard a remarkable story. One of them was married to a man who had just returned to Georgia for a high school class reunion he never dreamed he would be invited to, let alone want to attend. He had been bullied something fierce as a teenager. It had to do with civil rights and a communal farm and the demons of bigotry that had to be exorcised in the South and elsewhere.

"I thought it sounded like your kind of story," Ann said.

It was. I've written about many topics over the years, from religion to politics to food, but I've always gravitated toward stories about the intricacies of our race relations. Perhaps it's because I'm a fifth-generation Georgian who came along during the Civil War centennial years, which coincided with the height of the Civil Rights Movement, both of which unfolded momentously in my hometown of Atlanta. This particular story struck my tuning fork so resolutely that I turned it into a book: "The Class of '65: A Student, a Divided Town, and the Long Road to Forgiveness." As that title implies, I found more than demons in this true tale; I found the promise of change and reconciliation — a message of hope that, given recent events in Charleston, South Carolina, we need now more than ever.

Here's how it came about.

When Ann mentioned the name of the communal farm, I recognized it instantly: Koinonia (pronounced

COY-na-NEE-ah), a Greek word that means fellowship. Koinonia is known today as the birthplace of Habitat for Humanity, the nonprofit housing ministry, which evolved from an experimental program at the community during the late 1960s, but it had a very different reputation before that. There was a time when Koinonia was one of the most controversial and persecuted religious enclaves in the nation.

It was founded in 1942 near Americus, in southwest Georgia, by two white Baptist ministers and their wives who wanted to live simply, like the early Christians, sharing their resources and welcoming everyone in the spirit of brotherhood. In other words, they ate and lived with black people deep in the heart of the Jim Crow South.

Despite Koinonia's race-mixing ways, the locals mostly tolerated it for the first few years, as they might have put up with a nudist colony; they didn't approve, but they didn't get too agitated as long as no one paraded through town nekkid. That forbearance vanished in the mid-1950s when Koinonia's leader, the Rev. Clarence Jordan, spoke out on behalf of two black students who wanted to enroll at the Atlanta college that later became Georgia State University. Overnight, the commune became the target of vandalism and violence. Fences were cut and fruit trees chopped down. Koinonia's roadside market was leveled by a bomb. Businesses boycotted the farm's products and refused to sell it supplies. Klansmen shot into the property and snipers took aim at its houses.

That part of the story is fairly well known in certain religious, academic and journalistic circles. I knew it myself from visiting the farm in the fall of 1980, on my first out-of-town assignment for the Atlanta newspapers, when you could still see bullet holes in one of the older frame buildings.

The fresh aspect of the story — at least to me — concerned the children of Koinonia and the hell they went through when they entered the public schools just as the Civil Rights Movement was coming to a boil. One of those children was Greg Wittkamper, the husband of Ann's friend, who had the misfortune of being the only Koinonia kid at Americus High School the year it admitted its first black students, in the fall of 1964.

I phoned him in West Virginia, where he had lived for decades, and asked whether he would mind talking with me.

"How soon can you get here?" he said.

VOICES FROM THE PAST

Greg picked me up at the airport near the Greenbrier Resort, and we drove half an hour into a remote section of the Allegheny Mountains, where he lived in a rambling hillside house overlooking a pond where he sometimes went skinny-dipping. It was the summer of 2006 and he was almost 60, with gray patches in his beard. Now semi-retired from the real estate business, he was enjoying life with his second wife and their young daughter. He seemed a supremely contented man. But when we sat down on his wraparound deck to talk about his high school days, it didn't take long for the memories to bring tears to his pale blue eyes.

Greg is a preacher's son whose father moved the family to Koinonia in 1953 because he wanted to live among pacifists and back-to-basics Christians. When he began grade school, Greg was aware that other students regarded him as something of alien because of where he lived, but he didn't feel threatened until the night riders started attacking the farm three years later.

One night in 1957 stands out. He and some of the other children were playing volleyball when two cars slowed down on the highway and fired into the court area, sending the kids diving for cover. He vividly remembered seeing tongues of flame flicking from gun muzzles.

"We thought they were going to take us out and hang us on crosses," Greg told me in his soft, gentle voice.

The conflict between Koinonia and the outside community eventually moved into the public schools. The fellowship had to file a federal lawsuit in 1960 to force the city system to admit three of the farm's teenagers into Americus High, where authorities feared that their presence would cause trouble because the commune was an open supporter of civil rights. Greg enrolled there the following year.

All of the Koinonia children were harassed in high school, but none of them went through the hazing Greg experienced during his senior year. It started when he showed his solidarity with three of the students desegregating the school by riding to class with them in a limousine provided by a black funeral home. They were met by a mob throwing rocks and spewing hatred. Over the course of the school term, Greg was tripped, spat on, pushed down stairs, hit in the face with a sloppy Joe, called every ugly name in the book and shunned like a leper. He was physically assaulted on two occasions. True to his pacifist teachings, he never fought back.

The year ended much as it had begun. At graduation, in June 1965, Greg was booed as his name was called to collect his diploma, and then a couple of dozen ruffians chased him and his best friend, a young black man, off campus with more rocks and invective.

But something else happened at commencement that foreshadowed better days to come. One of Greg's classmates, who had become unsettled over the way he was being treated, walked up to him in front of everyone, shook his hand and congratulated him on surviving. His name was David Morgan. Decades later, he was the alumnus in charge of planning the 40th class reunion.

Greg had recently received a letter from David, the first communication they had had since that handshake. He went inside the house and came back with an envelope that contained three handwritten pages.

"I expect you will be quite surprised to hear from me," the letter began. "If you remember me at all, it will likely be for unpleasant reasons.

"I don't recall ever directly assaulting you, but I probably did to gain acceptance and accolades of my peers. In any case, I surely participated as part of an enabling audience, and tacitly supported and encouraged those who did. For that I am deeply sorry and regretful.

"Throughout the last 40-plus years, I have occasionally thought of you and those dark days that you endured at our hands. As I matured, I became more and more ashamed, and wished that I had taken a different stand back then. I knew, even then, that it was all wrong, yet I did nothing to stop it, or even to discourage it."

David's wasn't the only letter. Greg had a folder full of of them from people he had never expected to hear from again.

THAT'S MY HOMETOWN

I could have written a compelling book if I had done nothing more than document the way Greg, Koinonia and their friends in the black community were terrorized during the civil-rights era. That part, sadly, was predictable. The apology letters and the invitation to return for the reunion were unexpected. Seeking forgiveness for something that happened almost half a century before struck me as an extraordinary gesture. I wanted to understand it, to explore how these children of segregation had changed and why they wanted to apologize.

About a dozen classmates wrote or phoned Greg in the spring of 2006. They were not the ones who actually attacked him but were rather the "good kids" who had stood by and said nothing while the bullies — always a noisy minority — hounded him. Their silence reminded me of the white clergy that the Rev. Martin Luther King Jr. addressed in his letter from the Birmingham jail, the ones who knew right from wrong but seemed to prize order and tradition more than justice and morality. I wondered whether I would have been among the sheep if I had been a few years older and had been raised in Americus instead of Atlanta. Probably so.

I decided to focus on four classmates who had written the most heartfelt messages: two men and two women. They had all left Americus after high school and had their minds broadened by some combination of college, military service, change of locale or a deepening comprehension of their faith.

David, the reunion planner, had gone on to become a banker in Perry, Georgia. I visited him at his office and later at home and asked him to read his letter into my recorder so we could put it online with the initial feature story I did for the Journal-Constitution. It moved me to hear his eloquent words repeated in such a honeyed Southern accent.

One of David's pals in high school was Joseph Logan, the co-captain of the football team, who had become a professor at a community college in Enterprise, Alabama, where his attitudes evolved as he began to teach black students. When I went to see Joseph, he was in poor health and seemed to be in a confessional mood. He told me about a night on the streets of Americus when he joined a pack of white guys who assaulted a black man simply because they were angry about civil-rights protests. Joseph hadn't struck the man himself, but he nearly did, and he considered the moment an epiphany in his life. Joseph died before my book was published. I wish he could have seen how I used his powerful example of a young man finding his moral footing.

The two women I concentrated on had been best friends in high school. Celia Harvey Gonzalez, who was living outside Charleston, had married and moved away and then remarried a man of Spanish extraction who couldn't believe some of the stories she told him about life in Americus during segregation. Celia was particularly concerned about how I was going to portray her parents' generation, the adults who had defended the old racial order and tried to force Koinonia to leave the county, going so far as to launch a grand jury investigation of the farm as a communist front. She and I both knew that they wouldn't be heroes.

Celia's friend Deanie Dudley Fricks had written one of the most emotional letters to Greg. She was deeply religious and cited scripture about outcasts and persecution, even comparing the silence of her high school class to the silence of Christians during the Holocaust. I caught another glimpse of her sensitive nature this spring, a few weeks before the book came out, when she phoned me on the weekend of the commemorations of the Selma voting-rights marches. She had been watching TV in Albany, where she lives part of the time, and had seen a news program about the Leesburg Stockade, an infamous chapter of the civil-rights saga in which three dozen black girls protesting segregation in Americus were arrested in 1963 and held for weeks under primitive conditions at an antiquated stockade in the next county south.

"I can't believe that happened in my hometown and I never knew about it," Deanie told me. "Those girls were about my age. Why didn't I know about that?"

I tried to reassure her. I told her that I wasn't surprised she didn't know because she didn't go to school with those girls or go to church with their families. The local paper wasn't covering the protests, and most of the adults weren't talking about them in front of their children.

There was a long pause. I could tell Deanie was upset.

"That's my hometown," she finally repeated, "and I didn't even know."

FOUR OTHERS WHO STRUGGLED

Americus is a contradictory place whose history shows bright flashes of the Old South and the New South. A few miles north of town is the Andersonville prison camp, where almost 13,000 Union soldiers died of disease and exposure during the waning months of the Civil War. A few miles west is Plains, home of Jimmy Carter, whose election as president more than a century later wouldn't have been possible without the votes of millions of white Southerners and African-Americans. There are few places where the ghosts that still inhabit our region dwell in such close proximity.

When "The Class of '65" came out in April, Greg and I gave a talk to a large, appreciative crowd at the Carter Presidential Library in Atlanta and then drove to Americus for a presentation there. But first we headed out to Koinonia to visit the place that birthed the story. It's still there, on Highway 49, the old Dawson road, a working farm with some two dozen full-time residents and many more visitors who come like pilgrims to appreciate its history, its alternative take on Christianity and its dedication to organic agriculture.

Greg and I stood outside the cabin where his family used to live, identified by a sign as the "Wittkamper House." It was unseasonably warm and the gnats were already dive-bombing our ears. "Welcome to southwest Georgia," he said. We wondered aloud how the locals might receive the book. Greg had already heard of someone who had made a crack about how he wasn't interested because it was just something about "those communists."

We needn't have worried. The book was received warmly, thanks in part to a sympathetic front-page story in The Americus Times-Recorder. When we spoke that evening at the Lake Blackshear Regional Library, there was an overflow turnout that included several people from Koinonia, Habitat for Humanity and its spinoff, the Fuller Center for Housing. Some of Greg's classmates made it, including David Morgan, who had driven down from Perry. All four of the students who had desegregated Americus High in 1964 were there: Jewel

Wise, David Bell, Dobbs Wiggins and Robertiena Freeman Fletcher. I was pleased to see them, not just because they were an integral part of the story, but because their presence spoke to a question I had considered at length: What do we make of a civil-rights tale whose hero is white?

I didn't have to wait long for someone to broach the topic. In one of the first reviews of the book, in The Washington Post, columnist Donna Britt came right out and said it: "As a black person, I wondered: Was this another 'white savior' narrative — think of the movies 'Mississippi Burning' or 'The Help' — celebrating a white person's bravery for supporting beleaguered blacks while de-emphasizing the African-Americans who required courage just to survive? Wittkamper was horribly mistreated. So were his black schoolmates ..."

Perhaps I should I have paid more attention to the struggles of those four black students. I did tell their stories, but only in threads and patches. They were treated horribly, especially Robertiena, a bright, outgoing sophomore who had transferred from the black high school thinking that she could make some white friends if they would only be willing to talk to her. She was shunned as thoroughly as Greg. Then, near the end of her first year, she was arrested on a bogus morals charge — she had been caught in a car necking with her boyfriend — and had to study for her final exams in a jail cell. Despite that nightmare, she remained at Americus High and became the only one of the four who graduated there.

All that backstory was churning through my head during the question-and-answer session after our talk at the library. At one point, I located Robertiena in the audience and told her that her tribulations were worthy of a book in their own right.

"Don't worry," she said, smiling. "I'm thinking about doing one."

Robertiena recently retired as head of the pharmacy at the Houston Medical Center in Warner Robins and has more time on her hands now, so maybe she will write a book. I hope so. There are so many stories of pluck and bravery from those years. I told one of them.

Ultimately, that was enough for The Washington Post reviewer, who ended her meditation on the "white savior" question with this:

"But the more I learned about Wittkamper's grit, the more I admired him. Courage deserves acknowledgement no matter what color it's wrapped in. My predominant 'why' became 'Why can't the rest of us be as brave?'"

TURNING THE OTHER CHEEK

On the morning after our talk, Greg and I stopped by his alma mater to take a look around. Americus-Sumter County High School South, as it's now known, has changed substantially since the first black students walked through its doors in 1964. As integration progressed over the following years, most of the white families pulled out of the public schools and enrolled their children in a new private institution called Southland Academy, leaving Americus High almost 90 percent black. Years later, in a crowning irony, Robertiena's sister Juanita became principal.

It was a school holiday, and the doors were locked, but we were able to find an open gate and slip onto the grounds.

We walked toward the baseball grandstand, a green wood-frame relic of the 1930s, where one of the most dramatic scenes of Greg's time in high school played out. One of his classmates, Thomas, accused Greg of calling him a bastard and challenged him to a fight after school. Word spread that the kid from Koinonia was finally going to get his butt kicked, and when Greg tried to walk off campus, a pack of boys who wanted to see that happen stepped out from behind the grandstand and blocked his way.

"It happened about here," Greg said, stopping as if finding his mark on a stage. "They tell me there were about 50 boys, but it felt like the whole school was watching."

I assumed Thomas's role and faced Greg with my fists raised.

"So another boy came up from behind and knocked the books out of your hands," I said, picking up the narrative, "and that was when Thomas took a swing at you." I made a slow-motion arc with my right. "Exactly where did he hit you?"

Greg pointed to his cheek. "Right here. Hard. It almost knocked me down."

When I was writing about the showdown at the ballfield, I thought about the fortitude it took to get walloped in the face and not lash back in anger: the self-control, the commitment to nonviolence, the practical calculation that a counterpunch would invite others to join the attack. Now that I was confronting Greg with clenched fists, my viewpoint switched to Thomas' and what it must have felt like to throw that punch. I could remember only one time in my childhood when I had hit someone, a boy in the neighborhood, over some silly disagreement during a game.

I've never forgotten the white-hot flash of shame that surged through my head. It actually made me dizzy, as if I had been the one getting socked.

I told Greg about the encounter and how I instantly regretted striking another person. "It's a hell of thing to hit someone," I said.

Greg nodded. "I don't think Thomas really wanted to do it. He looked scared. I think he was just doing what he thought everyone wanted him to do."

As we stood there reliving the distant traumas of our youth, they didn't seem so distant, and I noticed that we both had tears welling up in our eyes.

MY PEOPLE ARE ELSEWHERE

The Class of '65 keeps getting its anniversary dates wrong. The 40th reunion that was the centerpiece of my book occurred 41 years after graduation. The first pass at a 50th reunion took place last year, 49 years after the fact, when several classes were hoping to hold a joint gathering in Americus. After those plans evaporated, some of Greg's class decided to get together anyway, and they enjoyed it so much that they scheduled another, larger reunion closer to the actual anniversary this year.

The 50th reunion of the Class of '65 was held three weeks after Greg and I went to Americus to speak at the library. I had planned to go back with him for the occasion, but several of the members I had interviewed politely asked me to reconsider. Their 40th reunion had been dominated by the reconciliation with Greg. Maybe this time, they suggested, we could leave them to each other's company without the reportorial attention and critical analysis.

I thought it was a reasonable request. I had already written about them welcoming Greg back to the fold. What else did I want — everyone to link hands and sing "Jesus Loves the Little Children"? As it turned out, there was another problem with my attending the reunion: Greg didn't really want to go.

He had his reasons. Americus is a long haul from his home in Sinks Grove, West Virginia — 560 miles. He had just made the 10-hour drive earlier in the month and wasn't looking forward to doing it again. More importantly, there was a grave illness in his family. His brother David, his closest sibling, who had accompanied him to the 40th reunion to watch his back, had Stage IV bladder cancer and was about to move into hospice in West Virginia. The whole time Greg had been in Georgia for the book launch, he was afraid that his phone would ring with bad news. It was a cruel twist that one of the happiest times of his life — seeing his story told in a book — would be tangled up with such creeping sadness.

But there was something else. Greg didn't especially want to go back to Americus for the 50th reunion because, to be honest, he didn't have much in common with most of his former classmates. He deeply appreciated their reaching out to him before the earlier reunion, and he did feel a closeness with several of the people who had led that rapprochement, such as David Morgan and Deanie Fricks. But he didn't feel a keen urge to see most of the others. He had made his peace with them — and they with him — and he didn't think there was much else to say.

Besides, there was another reunion this spring that he really did want to attend. After Greg graduated from

Americus High, he was accepted into Friends World College, an experimental Quaker program that sent students around the world to study other cultures. Now part of Long Island University, the school was holding its 50th anniversary celebration in New York City, hosting several hundred alumni at its Brooklyn campus, where they would be put up in dorm rooms.

On the last weekend in May, Greg joined his fellow Friends, many of whom came from alt-cultural backgrounds like his. Although most of them were far younger, they still wanted to know about what had happened to him in Georgia during the civil-rights era and about the book that laid it all out. To them, he was living history, a participant in one of the great social movements of the 20th century. To him, they were kindred souls who felt much more like his true classmates.

"These are really my people," he said.

A LONG ROAD TO TRAVEL

While Greg was flying to New York for the Friends World reunion, I was back in southwest Georgia speaking at the Albany Civil Rights Institute, a museum celebrating the movement that in 1961 launched some of the first mass protests against segregation anywhere. So many people were arrested that the authorities ran out of jail space and had to send detainees to surrounding counties — which is how Martin Luther King Jr. came to spend two nights behind bars in Americus. Koinonia was part of that saga; activists considered it a safe haven and used to hang out at the farm and hold orientation sessions there.

As I was preparing my talk, I heard from a woman in Americus who had opened the town's first bookstore in years, a place called Bittersweet, a nod to the fact that it also serves coffee and chocolate. Elena Albamonte told me that the shop's first sale had been a copy of "The Class of '65." She wanted to know whether I would be willing to stop by for a meet-and-greet after my appearance in Albany. Of course, I said.

I had been at the bookstore an hour when I noticed a vaguely familiar face approaching the signing table. It was Lorena Barnum Sabbs, president of the Barnum Funeral Home, one of the oldest and largest black-owned businesses in town. I had spoken with her several years before, and although she is not mentioned by name in the book, she is closely connected to its events. Her family provided the funeral home limousine that took Greg and the black students to Americus High on the day they were met by a mob in 1964. A year later, it was Lorena's turn to face the scorn as she started at the school and endured the same sort of daily harassment and name-calling that Greg and the others had put up with. She stuck it out and graduated in 1969.

Lorena told me that had she bought half a dozen copies of the book and given them to her children and other family members in the hope that they would remember where they had come from. I thanked her and asked whether any white graduates had ever apologized to her for the way she had been abused.

"A woman came up one time and said she couldn't believe the way they had acted toward us. She said it was a shame because we might have been friends under other circumstances."

"Did she apologize?" I asked.

"Not really."

I remembered Lorena telling me that she used to run into people around town who had mistreated her in high school. I wondered if that still occurred.

"Not a month goes by that I don't see one. In fact, I saw one here tonight in this bookstore. They usually act like nothing ever happened."

I wish I could report that the black students who were badgered like Greg had experienced the kind of reconciliation he has, but I cannot. With a precious few exceptions — one of which plays a crucial role in the book — it has not come to pass.

"I don't want you to get the impression that I think about this history all the time," Lorena continued. "I don't. I love this town, and I know we're going to get better. But we've still got a long way to go."

As she was talking, I glanced at the front window and saw the bookstore's name in a new light. How appropriate, I thought: Bittersweet.

— *Jim Auchmutey spent almost 30 years as a writer and editor for The Atlanta Journal-Constitution, specializing in stories about the South and its history and culture.*

First Published February 18, 2014

This Train is Bound for Glory, This Train...

•••

FLETCHER MOORE

This train... Carries saints and sinners
This train... carries losers and winners
This Train... carries whores and gamblers
This train... carries lost souls

—

Bruce Springsteen,
"Land of Hope and Dreams"

I'm sitting in the kitchen of a man who says he's died three times. Four, if you count an 85-year prison sentence he tells me he received at the age of 12.

There is no good reason Shawn Hubbard should be sitting here, but somehow he dodged every bullet. And now he's across the table from me, and I'm looking into his intense brown eyes beneath the perfectly trimmed Mohawk running along the crown of his head as he tells me that he's a second lieutenant in New Orleans' Gypsy Wolf Pack, and that the house is well-stocked with weapons, and that he and his friends could take probably 60 attackers before succumbing themselves, and for a split second, as his girlfriend — busy making a birthday cake for their nanny — pulls a hot skillet out of the oven, I'm visited by a sudden vision of her driving its searing iron mass through the all-too-flimsy wall of my right temple.

An hour later I'm eating a big alligator sausage on a slice of Bunny Bread. Fourteen hundred dollars' worth of meat — purchased entirely with food stamps — sizzles on a cinder-block grill the size of a Volkswagen Beetle, and a dozen odd-looking people sit in dingy plastic chairs swilling beers, smoking pot, petting a series of sleepy pit bulls and admiring the tiny pink child bouncing in a Johnny jumper just above the center of the dirt yard.

I gravitate toward Neil, a comparatively plain man in a muted red T-shirt and knee-length shorts, a mass of black hair attempting vainly to escape from beneath his baseball cap. He's intelligent and well-spoken, if roaring drunk; less inclined to fall into the litany of inside jokes and relentless sarcasm that animates the rest of the party. We discuss his journeys — he's hopped freights and walked all over the country, from Detroit to the Florida Keys to New Orleans. If you live in a big city you've probably seen people like him — weather-stained leather tramps and train kids gathered in grimy circles on downtown sidewalks. His like are outcasts, by choice, but their tales are powerful.

Toward the end of the evening, talking to Neil in the dark, he tells me that New Orleans always takes something from you, but that it also always gives something back.

What have I lost? And what have I gained?

THE WRECK OF THE
OL' BEST FRIEND

I'm headed southbound on that Southern Crescent Line,
going back to Alabama to see that gal of mine.

—

Tony Townsend, "Southbound"

A week prior to that memorable evening, I was perched on a barstool at O'Malley's Sports Pub & Grill, next door to the Dulles Airport Best Western in Sterling, Va., testing my capacity for IPA and tedium. Northern Virginia — the bits of it near Dulles International Airport anyway — is a cultural catastrophe the like of which hasn't been seen since the Library of Alexandria went up in flames. You can still spot the shriveled remains of the natural beauty that made it a place worth fighting a civil war over — a horse barn quietly rotting next to a Chevron, a stunned doe peering out of a small stand of trees at the eight-lane freeway between her and the next sliver of wilderness. These dribs and drabs, however, serve only to make the total effect that much more melancholy.

Lucky for me I wouldn't be sticking around. The following day I would board the Amtrak Crescent, bound for

New Orleans, and in so doing, retrace the paths of countless other travelers over the past 140 years.

Anyone who has spent sufficient time with me knows that sooner or later I will start waxing nostalgic about trains. I loved them as a kid, waving at the engineers across the highway from my grandparents' yard, and I love them as an adult, or I would if we still had any. Rail freight is a huge concern in the United States, but passenger service is like the Ernest Borgnine of travel options. Likely, more people downloaded the "Crazy Train" ringtone in the last couple years than actually rode a train, crazy or otherwise.

I'm not afraid of flying, but the novelty wore off when I was in my teens, and now I view it as a necessary evil, like colostomy bags. Driving isn't a whole lot better. I don't even call it driving; I call it nodding off and careening into a ditch. Alas, I can't get where I want to go via rail, so I haven't given it much thought other than the occasional lament. And that's the way it was until this past December, when a friend came back from a trip on the Crescent and reminded me what a joy it is to simply be on a train. So I figured I'd give it a spin.

The Crescent has a long and storied history, stretching all the way back to Christmas Day, 1830. On that day in Charleston, S.C., less than 20 years after Napoleon swept across Europe with nothing more than foot soldiers and horses, people began to enjoy the first regular passenger-rail service in the United States. A primitive steam engine called The Best Friend of Charleston, looking like nothing so much as a jumbo homemade barbecue smoker, whizzed along with its load of goggle-eyed commuters at a blistering 25 miles an hour — until the boiler exploded in July of the following year, blasting a fireman out of existence and giving us a word, "trainwreck," that still does yeoman's work describing out-of-control drunks — and most business meetings, if we're being honest.

The Best Friend traversed a mere six miles of track, but it was one of hundreds of lines that got hoovered up by the Richmond & Danville Railroad between 1847 and 1894. The R&D would play a major role in the Civil War, serving ultimately as the last supply line between Richmond and the rest of the Confederacy. A valuable strategic target, the railroad was devastated, but recovered quickly after the war and ultimately grew into a behemoth of the rail industry east of the Mississippi, finally comprising some 3,300 miles of track in nine states. In 1870 the R&D began passenger service between New York and New Orleans, a route it called the Piedmont Air Line, presumably because the train flew from city to city in a mere 58 hours. By the mid-1890s, the volcanic growth of the R&D proved to be more than the company could handle. Bankruptcy and receivership followed, then purchase by Southern Railway, which continued the Air Line as the Crescent, and later the Southern Crescent.

To say that the Southern Crescent was iconic is to do injustice to the word. In its heyday before the arrival of the interstate-highway system or of inexpensive flight, rail was the most civilized way to cover significant distances, and Southern Railway didn't skimp. The Crescent was one of the great historical travel experiences, akin to those 747s with the piano bars. The dining cars were first-class restaurants, and trains came equipped with club cars, domed observation cars and even library cars for a while. It's almost hard to imagine living in a world where people aren't just meat to be moved from place to place as cheaply as possible, but for a brief shining moment, that was the case. The train was not just a means of transportation — it was a place to actually be.

The sight of the forest green Ps-4 locomotives that pulled the Crescent from the mid-'20s to the early '50s is a breathtaking one even still. Engine 1401 resides in the Smithsonian Museum of American History, dominating the travel exhibits like the implement of some forgotten civilization of giants. The appeal of locomotives from late in the steam era is unlike that of any other vehicle. Modern diesels are streamlined boxes, all of the machinery hidden beneath a sleek hood, while for engines like the 1401, appearance is emphatically a statement of raw power and purpose. The huge spoked wheels and their heavy steel drive rods seem to have been discovered atop mountains rather than manufactured. The surfaces are all masked by a writhing tangle of pipes and mysterious cylinders. It's difficult to reconcile these machines with the environmental problems we face today (a 150-mile run required the burning of 16 tons of coal), but it's hard not to admire the industrial strength they radiate.

This particular engine hauled Franklin Delano Roosevelt's funeral train. That's a bygone era for sure, but if I were a raging egotist with far too much money — like, say, Donald Trump — I couldn't think of a better way to obsequiously mark my own death than to have my corpse hauled around the country in this manner.

I won't bore you with the series of acquisitions and mergers that led, ultimately, to the duopoly on freight east of the Mississippi by Norfolk and Southern and CSX. Nor will I dwell on the gradual decline of passenger rail other than to say that despite the frequent criticism Amtrak receives from the Adam Smith posse, I for one am glad they were there to pick up the pieces. Without them there would be nothing left. It's like the transportation version of the National Endowment for the Arts, nurturing those pieces of American culture too oddly proportioned to do well in a cutthroat marketplace but clearly possessing real value.

But what form does that value take? That's what I aimed to find out.

The plan was to board the train in D.C. New York was the other possible starting point, but this is The Bitter Southerner after all, and not The Bitter Northeasterner. Moreover, if there's any faith left in rail in the U.S., it resides in the Northeast Corridor, plus possibly California. Those people don't need to be told about trains.

The South, on the other hand, has a naturally contentious relationship with rail. Despite its weird centrality to the narrative of "Atlas Shrugged," rail is the antithesis of the individualistic spirit that so often characterizes Southern life, whether it be the cry of "states rights" that led wealthy, successful and otherwise intelligent people into a catastrophic war, or the modern libertarianism that leads wealthy, successful and otherwise intelligent people to cast ballots for Bob Barr. Rail does not allow for individual choice. Train passengers are a community literally on rails, all going to the same places at the same times, sharing tables at prescribed mealtimes and sleeping side by side in packed coaches (except the smattering of people in the wildly overpriced sleeper cars of course). Rail was once, out of necessity, the circulatory system of the whole region, but the trains are almost all gone now. Perhaps it was that Southern individualism that made us an easy mark for car salesmen.

Whatever the case, D.C. would be the departure point, and at the end of the line, New Orleans would be the destination. Along the way I'd make two stops, one in Danville, Va., and one in Meridian, Miss. I chose these two cities for reasons both historical and cultural. If you want a picture of the modern life of a venerable rail line like the Crescent, you could choose pretty much any city along the way, but Danville and Meridian loom large over the route, as you will likely agree when their stories unfold.

Lastly, I'd have a companion. The gods know that, left to my own devices, I'm prone to silence and self-isolation, so they sent me Artem Nazarov, a preternaturally talented photographer who shares my appreciation for fleabag motels and beer. Artem could charm a steak out of a cow, and his energy rarely flags as long as he's kept jittery with coffee. He's Russian, as everyone reminds him the moment he opens his mouth, but he doesn't take people's curiosity as patronizing, or at least he's smart enough to pretend not to. Instead he uses it to get up in their faces with his camera and take those otherworldly photos he makes. I was jazzed. We were well-armed. We were going story hunting.

GOOD TRAIN MEAT

And then a telegram come from Washington Station,
This is how it read,
"Oh that brave engineer that run '97,
is lyin' in Danville dead."

—

Fred Jackson Lewey / Charles Noell / Henry Whitter, "Wreck of the Old '97"

The first leg of the trip was to be a short one — a mere four hours from D.C. to Danville. I boarded the train at 6:30 in the evening. Artem was dealing with an emergency in Atlanta and had missed his flight but assured me he would meet me in Danville the next day. The train rolled out of the station illuminated by a sinking sun, and until the dining car opened I sat contentedly by the big picture window watching the the long shadows creeping across D.C.'s suburbs.

Eager for a train dinner, I plunged into the kitchen by accident. A cook, legs spread wide against the rocking of the train, struggled to extract something from the Stygian mouth of an oven just inches from his face, stumbling slightly as the car's trucks thumped over a turnout. It was like watching a gun crew feverishly working their piece on the pitching deck of a ship during the Age of Sail.

I lurched into the narrow corridor to the left of the kitchen's pandemonium and into the dining area. Amtrak's dining cars are still quite redolent of rail's zenith. I was met by a gracious host who led me directly to a white-draped table, already occupied by a trim man in his late 50s with a ballcap bearing the logo of a camping gear manufacturer. I should note at this point that there are doubtless those among you who would say that being arbitrarily matched with a strange dinner companion is not a characteristic of a five-star restaurant, and that may be true, but part of the genius of train travel is the collective experience that emerges if you let it. Especially if you're traveling alone, you are going to share a table with someone, and they are very likely to be as weird as you, and before the night is over, you will be knocking back beers with your new friend in the lounge and getting way too loud discussing politics.

My table mate was Andy. He was as good a fellow to spend several hours with as I could have wished. He was a hiker and a salesman, in precisely that order, and he was on his way to Georgia for a solid month of hiking alone in the wilderness. We conversed politely over pretty decent steaks ("good train meat," he said), and wound up meeting again in the lounge car a short while later, where we did indeed make a good-sized dent in the train's alcohol supply. We got loud, talking not just politics but music, salesmanship, family and trains. The latter, he assured me, was the vastly superior means of travel, not least because he could bring pretty much whatever he liked on the train with him. I'm pretty sure he was carrying a giant bag of weed. Pot would turn out to be a significant concern of a great many Amtrak riders, at least by my sampling.

I arrived in Danville at around 11:30 p.m., right on the heels of Jefferson Davis, give or take 150 years. A bit of history is in order:

On April 2, 1865, Robert E. Lee, who had spent nine months besieged outside Petersburg, Va., was finally forced to fall back. The Confederate government at Richmond, in imminent danger of being surrounded, fled to Danville by the only remaining railway, the Richmond & Danville. This was not precisely the same line as mine — at various times the R&D provided service both through Richmond and through Lynchburg, farther west. But when I stepped off the platform that night, I was following Davis.

Danville was, in fact, celebrating the anniversary that very night, with an antebellum ball downtown. Jefferson Davis' great-great-grandson Bert Hayes-Davis had been in town that afternoon, speaking at the Sutherlin Mansion — the home of a wealthy industrialist which served as the Confederacy's last capital. I discovered this too late, unfortunately. I would only be able to scour the town for reminiscences of his passing.

Another passenger getting off in Danville offered me a ride, sparing me the mile-and-a-half walk through the dark emptiness of the warehouse district. So just a short while before midnight I strode into the Hotel Leland in the center of downtown, two blocks from the Dan River.

It would seem that the only person in the entire world with anything substantial to say about Hotel Leeland is a semi-anonymous blogger named Jaded Lens, who captures the feel of the place with great veracity, "If Sid Vicious had died in Danville, his body would've been found in Room 21 of the Hotel Leeland." The place is a kaleidoscope of weirdness, and it hits you full force from the moment you walk through the door.

The lobby was a big, mostly empty room with wood paneling and inexplicable nautically themed paintings and objets d'art distributed along the walls. A couple banks of chairs lurked in various corners in case you wanted to enjoy the ambience at your leisure. At the rear of the room, to one side, was a largish wooden box with a counter and a glass window, behind which a corpulent and balding hotelier eyed me with suspicion. Behind him were an array of cubbies corresponding to the hotel's rooms. Some had keys; a few appeared to contain telegrams — probably sent to the occupants during the Great Depression and never delivered. There was also a small black-and-white television which was unmistakably displaying a signal from 1958.

I paid $32 for the room, but $5 of that was a key deposit. The clerk told me that it was cheaper to pay for a week in advance. As I filled out the registration form, two women in billowing black antebellum ball gowns swept past me and up the stairs.

I followed them as far the third floor, where my room was located. The staircase and the hallway were both symphonies of squeaking boards, and in places, the floor gave just enough to make me wonder if I might wind up putting a foot through it. Everything reeked of stale cigarettes — indeed, amid a jumble of broken furniture stacked in the hallway was a half-full ashtray.

The room itself was another anachronism. There was neither a television nor a bathroom — this despite the fact that the hallway was simply alive with televisual clamor. There was a sink: an antediluvian porcelain bowl with separate hot and cold taps. A lonely mirror hung over it. The furnishings were a mishmash — a hulking particle-board box that served as a wardrobe, a low but extremely long dresser that did double duty as a nightstand and a bar against the door to the adjoining room, a sagging chair that looked like it'd been stolen from the waiting room at a tire store, and a tiny, very thin bed with a puke-brown blanket, two cardboard pillows, and a cardboard sheet.

I dropped all my gear on the floor, lay down on the bed, and was suddenly serenaded by the theme from "Bonanza" twanging loudly from the neighboring room.

The next day was Easter. This fact was residue of my somewhat poor planning, but in the end it worked out. Artem wouldn't arrive until the afternoon, so I had several hours to do what I love best — walk around aimlessly. I rose and showered in the bathroom down the hall, a room which appeared to have been constructed out of scraps of other rooms, and headed out in search of breakfast, which I was fortunate to find just a block away: A chain restaurant called Biscuit World was doing brisk business with heathens.

Fortified, I spent the bulk of the day hiking around town. Danville was silent and empty. Much of the downtown area consists of empty, dilapidated tobacco warehouses. All of the mills that used to serve as the city's economic base are long gone, leaving nearly a third of the occupants in poverty. At 45 miles from the nearest interstate, it's hard to see how this will ever change.

Not that they aren't trying. I spent a couple hours hiking a pedestrian trail that runs alongside the Dan River on the north and east sides of the city. Clear blue skies and cool temperatures made the walking easy, and bright sunshine brought a vast profusion of turtles out onto logs and stones in the river, thick as roof shingles. One could almost forget that this was the same Dan River into which Duke Energy spilled 27 million gallons of coal-ash-contaminated water a year before.

At length I arrived at Dan Daniel Memorial Park. (Danville's Dan Daniel Park. Say that five times fast.) The 170-acre park is lovely, with ball fields, trails, a skate park, a large veterans' memorial and the ballpark of the Danville Braves — the advanced rookie affiliate of the Atlanta Braves.

Where does Danville get the money to build this sort of stuff? I don't know. Maybe it was cheaper than it looked, but one would think a skate park wouldn't be a high priority for a city in dire straits.

I returned to the Leeland at 3 that afternoon to find that I'd been checked out. Something about failing to paying for a second night. I settled and the hotelier accompanied me up to remove what amounted to a boot on the door handle. We rode a dilapidated lift stolen from an Indiana Jones movie. Exiting, we walked past the stairs into the hallway. A young black man was standing stock still about halfway up the staircase and muttering softly.

As we passed, he suddenly tumbled backwards down the stairs. He grabbed the door frame at the bottom which had the effect of redirecting him sharply through the doorway, around the corner and several feet down the hall. He crashed onto the floor, his cellphone flying in one direction and a bright green double-A battery flying another.

"Let me take you up on the lift, Ricky," said the clerk. Ricky declined, and mounted the stairs again. Perhaps it would be more proper to say that his feet mounted the stairs, as his upper body wasn't having any of it. He gripped the rail tightly with one hand — his other was employed holding his pants in a precarious position beneath his underwear — while his feet went on their merry way until finally he was suspended over the staircase at something like a 45-degree angle. The effect would have been comical were it not for the grim look on his face.

A second collapse being manifest, we sprang back to his aid. The hotel fellow repeated his offer of the lift, and I climbed up above him and begged him to accept assistance, but he was adamant. Whether from pride, or sheer stubbornness, or fear that something incriminating might pop out of a pocket somewhere, he was determined to make his own way up those baleful stairs. After a while I relented and tramped back down to the landing. As though I had triggered his snare, Ricky promptly fell over backwards on top of me.

Artem arrived shortly after the hallway comedy. We were both hungry and, everything around downtown being closed except Biscuit World, we ventured across the river to the west side, which is basically one of those strips of chain stores and plasticky restaurants that surround so many cities like a band of fat around the heart. Danville has one thing going for it at least, in that its ghastly nowhere-ville is confined to that one area. Unfortunately that's where most of the people seem to be as well. We ate at some anodyne family restaurant whose name I wouldn't be able to pick out of a lineup. Artem complained about the taste of the water, and I thought again about that coal ash spill.

After dinner we returned to the train station, an interesting place I'd seen only very briefly the night before. It's a small building with a central waiting area and two wings, one of which doubles as a science museum, or so the signs read. Really it's just a big taxidermy display, and not all of animals are native to the area, unless tigers once roamed southern Virginia. At one end of the building is a small room containing a largish model railroad layout under glass, and a bunch of Southern Railways memorabilia framed on the walls. A man in his late '60s or early '70s was there, and we got to talking. He was a "railfan." This is a term I'd encountered during my brief flirtation with model railroading as a kid, but I always thought it referred principally to modeling. Turns out, there's a rather startling array of activities that fall under the rubric, including modeling but also collecting-railroad related stuff; riding — or "bashing" — which consists of not simply riding but attempting to ride entire networks or visit every depot on a network; trainspotting — which is essentially the train version of bird watching; or any of a slew of other train-related hobbies.

My interlocutor had driven up from Greensboro to watch freight in Danville. It was a good spot, he explained, because he could get very close to the tracks. His knowledge about the history of rail in general and Southern Railways in particular was staggering. He knew many of the steam engines that had plied the Southern Crescent route particularly well, and talked to me about how their qualities were matched to the grades they had to climb, especially in North Carolina. He told me a great deal about the station in Danville — that it had been moved some 200 yards from its original position to the west, that the platform had once accommodated six rails (it's now just two). Of particular interest, he told me how diesel had devastated the economies of so many rail towns, since diesel engines required so much less maintenance than steam. The great Roanoke Shops, he told me, which produced almost 450 locomotives for Norfolk & Western between 1884 and 1953, were forced to conclude their business, and an army of highly skilled machinists suddenly found their talents worthless.

Sometimes I wonder if the world will become so efficient that none of us will have jobs.

THE DANVILLE MODEL
RAILROAD CLUB

Virgil Caine is the name, and I served on the Danville train,
till Stoneman's cavalry came and tore up the tracks again.
In the winter of '65, we were hungry, just barely alive,
May the 10th, Richmond had fell, it's a time I remember, oh so well.

—

The Band, "The Night They Drove Old Dixie Down"

When Robert E. Lee and his shattered army left Petersburg, their intent was to resupply and then march southwest into North Carolina, where they would join with the army led by Joseph E. Johnson. Their combined forces would seek to defeat Sherman to the south and then turn to face Grant in the north. All pure fantasy of course — Johnson's army was a tiny, ill-fed, ill-equipped, unpaid wreck, and Lee's wasn't much better. But it was on these plans that the final farce of the war unfolded.

Lee made for Amelia Court House, on the Richmond & Danville line, but when he arrived, there was no food to be had. Cavalry under Philip Sheridan had reached the line at Jetersville before the trains could get to Lee, and thus Lee's fate was sealed. He would surrender his army at Appomattox Courthouse a week later.

Robbie Robertson of The Band — a Canadian, mind you — wrote "The Night They Drove Old Dixie Down" about these events a hundred years later. The story goes that the Band's drummer, Levon Helm, an Arkansan, took Robertson to the library in Woodstock, N.Y., so that he could do due justice to the history. It's an awfully good song, but I'm not sure Robertson was really paying attention to those history books. The song has George Stoneman cutting the Richmond & Danville line instead of Sheridan. Stoneman was actually busy cutting the Virginia & Tennessee some distance to the southwest, as well as "dismantling the country" — as his orders read — for miles about and earning a fine reputation for himself among Confederate sympathizers as a Yankee monster. I'll grant Robertson poetic license though — Stoneman sounds better in song than Sheridan.

On Monday morning Artem and I dropped in at the Sutherlin Mansion, which was where Jefferson Davis and his cabinet alit after fleeing Richmond. The house, as previously mentioned, had the distinction of serving as the last capital of the Confederacy, though by that point the honor was transparently honorific. Davis' significant job duties while ensconced in Danville included eating, sleeping, making conversation with the Sutherlins, and going all bug-eyed when he was told that Lee's surrender was incipient. At least, that's how I imagined it as I stood in the dining room where Davis received the bad news.

The mansion is a gorgeous old jewel in the midst of a battalion of competitors — sprawling homes of sometimes breathtaking design. Many of them have been restored, but many are beset by decay, suggesting once again a certain spottiness to Danville's wealth. The Sutherlin in any case is in prime condition, and has served as the Danville Museum of Fine Arts and History since 1974, mostly housing artifacts related to Davis' stay there. The place is understandably enthusiastic about Davis, but also hosts a startlingly sympathetic display enumerating the arguments in favor of flying the Rebel flag. The museum flies the third flag of the Confederacy — not the stars and bars. I think the intent is to temper the sharp edge of the debate, but the effect is, at least potentially, one of deliberate obfuscation. I can't understand why they just don't cram all of it into a display case somewhere with a nice clear caption beneath.

Anyway, we took pictures and perused the gift shop — where I found myself spending an absurd amount of money on a badly typeset book about Danville during the Civil War. We pigeonholed one of the museum's officers, a kind gentleman of middle age with long graying hair and beard. He was the picture of a Confederate citizen except for the earrings.

He knew Danville inside and out, and told us pretty much every detail short of the color of the bedrock. We nodded politely, gandered at the various bits of furniture where Davis had done this or that, and, once we felt our brains would hold no more information about who owned this house or that one, when they sold it and to whom, we fled, like Davis himself.

We spent the balance of the afternoon wandering through the national cemetery with its hundreds of lonesome white stones standing at perfect attention like the soldiers buried beneath them, and shooting photographs of the empty warehouses and the rail yard near downtown. Artem hit the road around 4 p.m. with the aim of getting himself and his car back to Atlanta in time to get a few hours' sleep before meeting me for the ride to Meridian. I had seven hours to kill, so, with nowhere to go and nothing to do, I whiled away the hours with beer and pizza in a little place downtown.

Looking back, I should have just stuck around until closing time. As it was, I had picked up word from a poster sighted in a shop window that the Danville Model Railroad Club was meeting around the corner. Leaving my stuff, I dashed off to check. I met a man outside the building where their meetings took place and he assured me that they'd be there until 10. So I returned to the restaurant, paid the bill, gathered up my things and headed out. This time, even though it was only a quarter of an hour later, the building was pitch dark and not a soul was to be seen. I called the number he'd given me — it led to a disconnection message. In my frustration and mystification, I then managed to drop my phone on the sidewalk. A thick spiderweb of cracks spread from one corner across every inch of the screen.

Vexed, I stomped off to the train station. I was something like two hours early, and the waiting room was inexplicably locked, so I camped out in the old caboose they had sitting out back as a novelty and spent the time watching "Spinal Tap" on my wounded phone. To make matters worse, the train was a good hour late, so by the time it finally arrived, the warm influence of the beer and pizza was a long distant memory. I was exhausted and feeling quite put upon by the universe.

I was perhaps not in the best state of mind for what came next.

VILLA RICA, TEMPLE, WACO, TALLADEGA

And the train conductor say,
Take a break driver eight,
Driver eight take a break,
We've been on this shift too long.

—

R.E.M, "Driver 8"

When I think of train travel, I tend to think of Cary Grant and Joan Fontaine in "Suspicion." Everybody is overdressed, sitting in positions designed to maximize their physical appeal — yet they never experience any discomfort. There's no stretching or squirming around in the seat. Nobody has greasy hair or is wearing three-day-old shirts. Nobody is pulling wedged underwear out of unmentionable crevices. Nobody is lurching around the car in a vain quest for the bathroom.

Maybe it was like that in the old days. I don't know, but it sure as hell isn't like that now. I hate to be the one to spoil anyone's fantasies, but the honest truth is that in many regards Amtrak is running buses on rails. And I was about to spend an entire night on one.

On boarding, I was placed — via Amtrak's incomprehensible seating scheme, which forces everyone to sit clumped as closely as possible — next to Jesse, a tattoo artist from Danville. He was returning to Gulfport, Miss., having come home to Danville to visit his family. We talked briefly. I asked him about all of Danville's improvements, and his only remark was that improving Danville was like painting poop.

As the train got moving I noticed that there were a lot of empty seats behind us. Jesse was decent company, but why, I thought, should I not just grab an entire empty pair and stretch out a little bit? So I did.

Inside of five minutes a porter was asking me if I'd been assigned that seat. I figured lies would be the best policy, so I replied, innocently, "Yes." He fiddled around with some papers and walked away. Ten minutes later another porter stopped by to ask me the same question. "Yes," I stated flatly. Another 10 minutes, another porter. I prepared to continue my fiction, but instead of asking me anything, he proceeded to harangue me, "I didn't assign you to this seat." I shrugged. He told me that if a family got on he'd have to move me. I shrugged again, but I was starting to feel like an asshole.

No families boarded the train that night, but in Greensboro a large Native American man sat down next to me and immediately began to snore loudly.

It was a horrible night. Maybe it's just me — I simply can't sleep in a non-horizontal position. Every 20 or 30 minutes

I would slump sufficiently far enough in one direction or another to put myself in danger of either asphyxiating or breaking my neck. Even when I managed to get semi-comfortable I tended to wake up periodically with a sudden start out of a fear of sliding into my neighbor's lap.

So the entire night passed as a series of short, shallow naps. Every now and again the train would arrive at some station and the porters would come through as loudly as possible to unload old passengers and load new ones. It being North Carolina, I remember being vaguely aware, during the brief, delirious periods between dozing, that I was probably missing some of the best scenery on the whole route.

At some iniquitous hour even the Amtrak people seemed to realize I wasn't really going to sleep, so they abruptly switched on all the lighting in the car and shouted over the intercom that it was breakfast time in the dining car. Craving a change of scenery, I went. On the way I noticed that Jesse had managed to keep my vacated seat and was stretched out across both of them, snoring contentedly.

I breakfasted with another ball-capped single man — a retired dentist this time — who also groused about the wretched condition of these United States, especially as concerned the legality of marijuana. He was a nice enough fellow, but much more standoffish than Andy. I suppose a night spent bent into the shape of a question mark shape with your face pressed against a window or hanging over an armrest will do that. I enjoyed the conversation well enough, and the food was, once again, not bad for train meat, but I was quite ready to put a cap on it as the Atlanta train station trundled into view.

Artem wasted no time belittling me for my complaints about the discomfort of the previous night. For whatever reason, almost everyone got off the train when he got on — I'm sure it wasn't personal, but the cars were sparsely populated all the way to New Orleans and back. He marveled at the comfort and legroom of the coach seats and promptly took a nap in one of them, probably out of pure Russian spite. I set up my "office" in the lounge car — laying claim to a whole table and spreading my notebook and other odds and ends across it — and proceeded to watch while western Georgia and eastern Alabama scrolled past the window.

For scenery, this was the best part of the journey. Once the suburbs and seedier towns in Atlanta's dingy penumbra were gone, the land crumpled into steeply wooded hills blanketed in last year's leaves. Every now and again a river or creek would appear underneath the train, and on the sharper curves I could see the cars ahead of me glittering in the dappled sunlight. We passed through a series of hamlets which each betrayed their rail-centric history with a strip of businesses facing the tracks — Villa Rica, Temple, Waco — and then, after crossing the Alabama state line, we dove into the Talledega National Forest. An idyllic field split by a creek in a stone race. Steep ridges and plunging ravines. Untrammeled creek valleys. Six deer in a meadow, regarding us with static intensity.

The passage was too quick. In no time at all we were passing a band of heavy industry west of Anniston, then the creepy steel musculature of the Anniston Army Depot, and then long stretches of tin-roofed houses with heaps of disintegrated consumer debris in the backyards. The Sloss Furnaces rolled past like some Southern version of the La Brea Tar Pits. Birmingham and a smoke stop for Artem.

We had lunch with an older black man who was a retired chemical worker. He was riding home from Atlanta, where he'd been visiting his kids. Why the train, we asked? Tired of the hassle of airport security.

We talked to a man from New Orleans who works on a turtle farm — 20,000 turtles per pond. I don't know how many ponds, but even one would be more turtles than I expect I've seen in my entire life. He told us he preferred the train for the cost.

We met a Franciscan monk from Cullman, Ala., complete with a heavy brown robe and a chunky wooden cross around his neck. He stood out somewhat from the crowd. He was heading to Slidell, La. to pick up a used vehicle that had been donated to his monastic community. Why the train? Well, I almost didn't need to ask. How in the hell would you fly from Cullman to Slidell?

Convenience and cost. What a utilitarian nation we inhabit. It was exceedingly rare to hear anyone say they liked the train because it was a throwback to a simpler world, or that they liked the languorous unspooling of a trip, the sense of being someplace rather than just going someplace.

But then, most the people lonely enough to engage us in discussion were single men, and probably not the type given to poetic musings.

THE MERIDIAN BASSOONIST'S SOUTH

My pocketbook is empty and my heart is full of pain
I'm a thousand miles from home just a-waiting for a train

—

Jimmie Rodgers, "Waiting for a Train"

Meridian is the quintessential railroad town. It emanates from the rail yard like wings on a butterfly — the quaint downtown grid on the north side, a band of light industry and chain businesses on the south. Like Atlanta, Meridian was born at the intersection of two major rail lines: the Southern Railway and the Mobile & Ohio. As such, Meridian was of significant enough strategic value during the Civil War to entice Sherman to march out of Vicksburg during a few spare weeks in February of 1864 and burn the place to its foundations. The Meridian campaign is considered by many to have been a warmup for the March to the Sea that Sherman would undertake across Georgia nine months later. In any event, it didn't endear Meridian to the man, and to this day it's no challenge to find Meridians who haven't quite gotten over it.

We checked into a cheap motel on the south side inexplicably called the Astro, where I enjoyed the civilizing effects of a hot shower before we caught a cab back into town. It took forever to show up (there are exactly four cabs in Meridian, and they will be on the far side of town no matter where you are) and when it finally did the driver had the stereo turned up so loud that any conversation was impossible. He dropped us off near the train station, and we began investigating.

To the extent that Meridian is withering (and my admittedly brief visit suggested it was), it seems to be withering from the outside in, rather than from the inside out, as so many cities do. There's a small core of vibrant activity just around the train station, a few lively bars and restaurants and stores. Beyond this center, it drops off sharply. The downtown possesses many beautiful but sadly empty old hotels in a semicircle a couple blocks out from the station. But after no more than a quarter mile the hard poverty begins to set in. Somewhere out there, in Meridian's suburban hinterlands, lies Peavey, the musical equipment manufacturer whose name has been synonymous with the city since the 1950s, until now. Even as we visited, Peavey was busy closing down its manufacturing facilities and relocating to China, landing another body blow to a place that may not be able to weather many more.

Yet Amtrak and the freight yard continue to pump blood into the heart of Meridian.

Mississippians seem to recognize this — that rarest of breed, the Republican rail booster, is fairly common in the state. Meridian itself can say that a former four-term Republican mayor, John Robert Smith, also served as chairman of Amtrak's board of directors. God knows the cards are stacked against the place, and against Mississippi in general, but in this at least there's a glimmer of hope. The people we met in that small pocket of life were mostly young — many of them students of Mississippi State, no doubt — and almost defiantly cosmopolitan. They are a seed in the throes of a terrible storm, and I couldn't help but root for them. I would go back to Meridian just to hang out with these people and drink their beer, I truly would.

Once we realized we couldn't spiral out very far, we spiraled back in and hit Weidmann's for a drink. Weidmann's bills itself as the oldest restaurant in Mississippi, and whether or not that is a fact, I liked it. It's an oak-paneling-and-mirrors sort of venue, with high ceilings and walls festooned with framed photographs of famous visitors, significant Mississippians, and historical images of the restaurant.

We ate dinner at the Brickhaus across the street. It was a bit cheaper, a bit more on the fried side, and it came with a bar sporting 63 taps. So we polished off the evening with a couple beers each at a table out front while the bartender periodically amused us by stepping out to take a drag on his homemade vaporizer, emitting six-foot long columns of smoke like some bearded, bespectacled dragon.

By the time we got back to the Astro, I was positively exhausted. It was about 10:30, and I recall turning on the TV and seeking out baseball. I sat on the bed, took off one shoe, and the next thing I remember was waking up in the same position to find the ballgame finished. I checked my phone. It was 12:30. So much for being unable to sleep in a non-horizontal position.

The next morning we made a beeline for the Jimmie Rodgers museum, located a couple miles north of downtown in Highland Park. We took another cab, which entailed both the staggering wait and ear-stabbing stereo levels. It must be a Meridian thing. Along the way, we discovered the other aspect of the city — row upon row of rotting hovels like dead mushrooms, with vegetation growing up around them and threatening to swallow them whole. The poverty set in like a cancer almost immediately past the compact downtown and didn't let up until we reached the park.

We arrived early, so we killed a half hour checking out the Dentzel carousel that is housed nearby. Manufactured by the Dentzel family — which was pretty much to carousels what the Stradivari family was to stringed instruments — for the 1904 St. Louis Exposition, the carousel was moved to Meridian in 1909. It's one of a kind, for reasons that will impress nobody but carousel junkies, but whatever its provenance or the historical qualities it may possess, it is manifestly a wonderful fusion of engineering and art.

Aside from the expected menagerie of zebras, horses, camels and lions, it features a wealth of original oil paintings all around its top. These are more weird than beautiful, but compelling in any case — they consist mostly of images of animals in their native landscapes, but also images of famous landmarks such as the canals of Venice and the Great Pyramids. The animals are often depicted in bizarre action poses — a bear fighting a giant snake, for example, or an alligator chomping down on a swan — and none of them appear to have been done from life, but rather from slightly inaccurate period secondhand sources. The effect is phantasmagorical.

The carousel is belt-driven off of a big electric motor inside a chunky cast iron case. It goes pretty fast and lurches somewhat as though it's not quite true on its axis. But we were game. We each mounted an animal, spent a few minutes spent hurtling in circles whooping and hollering a bit, and then, thanking the carousel guy, we headed back to the museum.

Jimmie Rodgers, of course, is a towering figure in American music. He's often referred to as the Father of Country Music, but his influence extends across many genres, including blues and rock. In his day job as a railroad worker on the Southern Railway, he learned his musical craft from other railway workers and hobos. His music is heavily influenced by the blues, meaning he (a white man) was basically Elvis-ing long before Elvis was even born. Rodgers was from Meridian, and the museum devoted to his life and his music is one of the highlights of the city. So we weren't going to miss it.

The building that houses the collection is modest, and you'll probably have to crank your understanding of that term down several notches to really get the gist of what I'm talking about. Picture your living room full of Jimmie Rodgers memorabilia.

Of that there is quite a lot. Guitars, old photographs, copies of old albums, dishware with Rodgers' face on it. There was a sizable collection of furniture, confirming that Rodgers sat like the rest of us. The guitars were interesting, in particular a beautiful old Martin with Rogers' name inlaid in mother-of-pearl on the fretboard. It was absolutely pristine, and kept so by a climate-controlled enclosure built into an old bank safe. My fingers itched to play it.

Probably the best thing about the place was the woman running it that day. An older woman with short grey-white hair in a bob, she wore a T-shirt with a picture of a man on skis in a cotton field. "Ski Mississippi," it read. She was enormously enthusiastic and helpful to a fault. When Artem became fixated on a CD recording of Marty Stuart playing Native American music, she cut the package open and put it on the stereo. And so we sauntered around for a while listening to drums and chanting and other non-Rodgers-esque sounds.

Most of the time we were in the building she busily sifted through piles of paper and old binders, looking for interesting material for us. When I mentioned that we hadn't had a chance to get any breakfast, she dug out a couple of packages of Pop Tarts. She reminded me of nobody so much as my own grandmother, God rest her soul.

When we expressed interest in the grave of the Gypsy Queen, Kelly Mitchell, buried there in Meridian, I'll be damned if she didn't drag us right out to her car and drive us there. We admired the half-dozen gypsy royalty graves, of which Mitchell's is the most obsequious. It was liberally mounded with beads, wine and liquor bottles, pennies, candles, hair ribbons, smokeless tobacco containers, jewelry, ashtrays, rotting fruit, plastic cups, beer cans, lighters, cigarettes, innumerable bits of unidentifiable trash, and rising like a monument in the middle, a five-gallon jug with a foam microphone windscreen over the mouth. It looked like the site of a particularly out-of-control party.

I hope I've established that the museum lady was kind and friendly, and that I bear her no ill will. For those reasons and more, it was acutely painful to me, when our discussion ranged to Meridian and its many ills, to hear her tell me in a hushed voice, that Meridian "had had problems with the blacks."

Another brief history lesson: In 1871 Meridian was the site of a series of race riots which began with a fire that burned down a large section of downtown. This same area had only recently been rebuilt after the destruction Sherman had wreaked seven years prior, and people were understandably upset. Unfortunately they let their passions get the best of them. The Republican mayor was blamed, and some days later, at a trial involving several of his political allies, a gunfight broke out in the courtroom, in which the presiding judge and several others were shot dead. The Mayor was driven from office, and over several days some 30 African-Americans were killed. The Meridian riot was a signal victory for Southern Democrats and the Ku Klux Klan. Mississippi would see the rise of other groups similar to the Klan, and ultimately, the reinstatement of Democratic politics. By the time Reconstruction ended in 1877, the tide was running strongly against the cause of freedmen. Indeed, their progress was set back significantly — almost a hundred years, as it would turn out.

So, if Meridian "had a problem with the blacks," I think it's fair to say that blacks had a problem with Meridian.

Anyway, I'm not sure which is more distressing: hearing this sort of thing spoken aloud, or witnessing myself pasting a strained, tight-lipped half-smile on my face in response. It's as though someone with a serious illness just threw up on my shoes and I pretended it didn't happen. Years ago, Eddie Murphy did a short film for "Saturday Night Live," in which he dressed in whiteface and went out to discover what life was like for white people. When a white newsstand owner gives him a newspaper, a light goes off:

"Slowly, I began to realize that when white people are alone, they give things to each other for free."

There's some truth in this. Even today, some folks will let down their guard when they think they are among their own, and out comes the little racist monster. I don't know what it's like to be black, but in moments like that, I don't want to be white.

Like all Americans, we as Southerners get to choose what to keep and what to discard from our lives. We are free to throw out heirlooms that are dangerous or foolish, and we are no less Southern for doing so, anymore than our ancestors risked losing their identity when they chose to lay steel rails across their land. We could all stand to do this. We could get rid of white flight, racial profiling, and the rebel flag. For my own part — in the interest of being the change I'd like to see — I'd be happy to get rid of that awkward politeness, a facet of Southern hospitality, that restrains me when white people try to give me things for free.

We ate lunch at Weidmann's that afternoon, and struck up a conversation with our waiter Stephen — a black man who was waiting tables until he was able to go back to music school in Hattiesburg. He was a bassoonist.

"I'll bet," I said to him, "you know some Stravinsky." Without hesitation he sang the bassoon line from "The Rite of Spring" in a perfect, buttery smooth baritone. Stephen was tall, handsome and charming, intelligent, talented and with a good sense of humor.

Who wouldn't want to live in his South?

THIS TRAIN CARRIES CHOOSERS

Roll Southern Crescent through the night,
Roll through the darkness through the light,
Roll all the way to New Orleans,
Want to eat a plate of rice and red fried beans.

—

Tom Dews, "Southern Crescent"

The ride from Meridian to New Orleans was blessedly brief and uneventful. We passed through Laurel, Hattiesburg, Picayune and Slidell, all of which are names that hold a certain fascination for me — they all sound deeply Southern. I always imagine that visiting them will involve a lot of sweet tea, cotton and blues on the front porch. I used to think the same things about Tishomingo, Corinth and Tupelo too, but I visited all of them and found them to be mainly like everyplace else — McDonald's, Walmart, Autozone and all the rest of it. I've never understood how people can defend all manner of crimes in the name of heritage and yet remain silent while this junk colonizes our storied towns and cities. Walmart isn't anyone's heritage.

Crossing Lake Pontchartrain was the highlight of this leg of the journey. The sun was sinking and the lake was lit in gold. To the west the shore was not visible — we could look out of the right-hand windows of the train and plausibly pretend we were at sea. To the east the shore was just the merest suggestion, but the I-10 causeway could be seen at a distance of 1,000 yards or so. The motion of the train and the low angle of the sun combined to make the water's surface look like a solid block of bronze.

As always with the best parts of the ride, it was over too quickly. The railroad causeway crosses at the neck between the big part of the lake on the west side and the small bulge to the east. It's the narrowest point. In no time we were passing through New Orleans, through the neighborhoods of Little Woods and Gentilly; through the city park and Greenwood Cemetery, like a city of the dead; and finally, slowly, into the Amtrak station just southwest of the French Quarter. End of the line.

This was to be our big night off, so after we settled into our rooms at the Empress Hotel — a place considerably more dreary than its name would suggest — we ditched the tools of our trade: Artem his cameras, I my notepad and a pocket full of pens. We found a bar in the French Quarter that served a superb bowl of red beans and rice. We ate and talked Coen brothers movies with a guy named Max. Max was a musician — a drummer who had relocated from Seattle in hopes of becoming a professional jazz player. He was a good conversationalist. I found myself reaching for my notebook.

We moved around through a series of bars on Frenchmen Street, listening to a procession of terrific bands. The ability of New Orleans to produce so much good music in such a small space on a Thursday evening cannot be overstated.

At the end of the evening we retreated back to the hotel. As we walked the last couple blocks we spotted a wiry figure dotted with tattoos and sporting a Mohawk. Next to him walked a woman, short and stout, wearing glasses and a pink T-shirt. She bore no signs of any social ties with him other than a small tattoo on one calf.

"Do you think he picked her up tonight?" Artem asked. Their proximity said they were a couple, but they didn't hang all over each other.

"No," I replied. "They've been together for a long time."

"Let's find out," he said, and then, to them, brandishing his Russian accent like a lasso, "Hey guys, what's your story?"

The guy stopped and turned, eyes flashing. This, I thought through a not-inconsiderable alcoholic haze, is a good way to get knifed. But Artem was talking, and countenances softened, and before we knew it, we were invited to a barbecue.

And now you know how I wound up, the following night, in the kitchen of a man who has died three times.

It's ironic, perhaps, that our trip ended with a group of people who have spent serious time riding freight trains. It's hard for me to endorse their lifestyle: living in squats, panhandling (some of them worked straight jobs, but panhandling is definitely a part of the life), and above all, fighting. I guess I'm a boring conformist like anyone else. I like owning a house, I like earning my own money, and I like not being stabbed.

Call me crazy.

Yet, a part of me admires their strident self-determinism. These are people who actually practice what I preach: Keep what they need and discard what they don't. My choices would be vastly different, but they've done something most of us don't. They've actually made choices.

And where their choices really cut me to the quick regards trains. In case I haven't been clear, I want trains. I want to see the South thickly crisscrossed by rail once again. It's the most civilized way to travel, and by God, it is as much the future as it is the past. Look no further than Japan for proof of that. Yet rail in the South hangs on by the slenderest of threads — namely the glorified bus that I'd just spent the last week riding for 1,000 miles.

And then, damned if I don't run into a house full of people who refuse to acknowledge the death of passenger rail in America. They just climb aboard the nearest freight and ride it like a bunch of 21st-century hobos. It's illegal and it's dangerous, but I can't help but thrill at the notion of people hacking new paths through the cultural and technological wilderness they inherited.

Earlier in the day we spent a half hour sitting on a curb watching a group of young musicians. There were at least seven of them altogether — a couple guitars, string bass, banjo, fiddle, lap steel and harmonica. None of them looked terribly clean or well-fed; I would guess they were living in situations not dissimilar from Shawn and his crew. Squatters probably, making their living entirely through busking. But they were cheerful and exuberant, and they spent their days simply playing music. No matter their problems, they spend most of their time doing something many people dream of.

We ran into a kid named Derek who was dressed like a cross between Huck Finn and Ruby Rhod from "The Fifth Element." He was an art student from Baltimore, looking to break into fashion design. I generally dress like I just found a pile of clothes in a parking lot, but this guy was charisma made flesh and I wish him well.

Walking through the French Quarter I was accosted by a corpulent old man who looked like nothing so much as Santa

Claus straining the seams of a pair of dirty black nylon pants and a barf-colored T-shirt. Spotting my Boston Red Sox cap and my Bitter Southerner shirt, he remarked in a booming voice, "Better to be a bitter Southerner than to be from Boston." Fair enough.

Like any large city, perhaps more so, New Orleans is full of unique people making their own unique ways. They've all recognized, consciously or otherwise, that a good life is just a question of figuring out what you really need and what you don't. It doesn't have to be what Shawn chooses, and it doesn't have to be what a bunch of street musicians choose. It doesn't have to be what Derek or Max the Drummer or Ignatius J. Reilly choose.

But it damn well isn't a prix fixe menu.

THE MISTS OF PONTCHARTRAIN

Well the Amtrak Crescent is a northbound train,
when you can't afford to stay no more in New Orleans.
So I bought the cheapest ticket and carried my clothes,
and the blood beneath my eyes from a broken nose.

—

Scott Miller, "Amtrak Crescent"

So what did I lose and what did I gain in New Orleans? Well, I lost my sunglasses somewhere, and in fact I did get a replacement from a Chevron booth at the French Quarter Festival. I suspect that wasn't what Neil was talking about, but the truth is, as much as I love the city, I'm hesitant to ascribe magical qualities to it. I spent most of a week either in tiny, quiet towns I'd probably never have considered visiting under other circumstances, or in a squealing steel box. Along the way I lost the old me. And I gained a new me — the difference between the two is expressed in the words you've read here, plus a couple dozen other stories for which I don't have room but which will leak out gradually at bars and dinner parties, probably repeatedly as I grow senile. I'd own just a fraction of that new me had I just driven from D.C. to New Orleans and slept at Marriott, though I'd have gotten there quicker. On the whole I'd say I came out ahead.

The ride back was anticlimactic, as return trips almost always are. It was a long day — some 13 hours spent entirely on the train. But the cars were almost empty, as though it had been a one-way trip and we'd simply gotten a behind-the-scenes view of the whole thing resetting to a new experience for the next group of adventurers.

There's not much to be said about that ride — Artem and I were both drained and I was urgently ready to be home with my family. But we did receive a last gift from the weather, which sent us a light rain as we recrossed Lake Pontchartrain. I watched the drops of moisture stream down the windows with the gray lake behind them, and each one seemed to refract the view of another person who had made the journey before me. Whether for purely pragmatic reasons, or for the romance of it all, or — stretching back far enough — because it was simply the only way to cover the distances involved, we all shared something distinctly American, distinctly Southern and unique in both its joys as well as its warts:

The Southern Crescent.

— *Fletcher Moore is a web developer working in Atlanta. He is not a writer by trade but is most assuredly a writer.*

First Published March 18, 2014

Kiss My Grits

◆◆◆

SHANE MITCHELL

Shane Mitchell hates grits. Thus, she is a heretic in her family, which has 325 years' worth of roots deep in grits country — Edisto Island, S.C., to be precise. So The Bitter Southerner asked the impossible of her: Go forth, Shane, and learn to love grits. This is her story.

> *"On every breakfast plate in the South there always appears a little white mound of food. Sometimes it's ignored. Sometimes insulted. But without it, the sun wouldn't come up, the crops wouldn't grow, and we would lose our drawl."*
>
> —
>
> Bill Neal, "Good Old Grits"

"Eat your grits."

"No."

"Don't you know?" asked my mother. "There are children starving in Africa."

"Not my problem."

"We don't let food go to waste in this house, young lady, so you will sit there until every bite is gone."

My mother, a beautiful redhead from Florence, S.C., knew this was an empty threat. We'd been at this kitchen table standoff over boiled-corn particulate before. Left on the plate long enough to congeal, either by accident or picky-eater pigheadedness, the breakfast bane of my childhood took on a disgusting texture: lumpy on top with a slimy underside like the exposed white belly of a dead snake flattened on the road. It made me gag, but there was a certain perverse pleasure to poking it with a fork.

I hate grits.

Buzzard poo. Spackling paste. Corpse skin.

As a cultural marker, this one sticks to the ribs of the region, so much that the states sandwiched between Texas and Virginia have been christened "The Grits Belt." Georgia declared grits its official prepared food in 2002. A similar bill was introduced in South Carolina:

"Whereas, throughout its history, the South has relished its grits, making them a symbol of its diet, its customs, its humor, and its hospitality, and whereas, every community in the State of South Carolina used to be the site of a grits mill and every local economy in the State used to be dependent on its product; and whereas, grits has been a part of the life of every South Carolinian of whatever race, background, gender, and income; and whereas, grits could very well play a vital role in the future of not only this State, but also the world, if as Charleston's The Post and Courier proclaimed in 1952, 'An inexpensive, simple, and thoroughly digestible food, [grits] should be made popular throughout the world. Given enough of it, the inhabitants of planet Earth would have nothing to fight about. A man full of [grits] is a man of peace.'"

Despite this geographic ubiquity, all grits aren't thoroughly digestible. Only recently I discovered that my distaste might have more to do with an inventor from Crystal Lake, Ill., than my parent's stovetop skills.

Instant grits probably seemed like a good idea at the time. If you were raised in a Southern family during the 1970s, a man named Roy G. Hyldon was largely responsible for what wound up being served at breakfast. Postwar convenience foods still dominated supermarket shelves; "heirloom" referred to your Nana's silver service; even brilliant cooks like my mother occasionally defaulted to a cardboard container emblazoned with the logo of a bewigged religious elder.

In 1967, Hyldon and his associate James T. Collins filed U.S. Patent 3,526,512 for perfecting "an instant food product of the corn grits type" for the Quaker Oats Co. The process as defined in the patent description involved admixing corn grits with polysaccharide gum and emulsifiers in order to create a product that can be prepared "by the mere addition of warm water … in a serving bowl."

Buried in the patent's technical lingo about "dried sheets of discrete particles in a starch matrix" is this unappetizing paragraph:

Still another advantage of our new combination of additives becomes apparent after the product is prepared for use. When conventional corn grits are prepared in large quantities and stored on a steam table or the like to keep them warm until serving, they soon become an adhesive mass or cake and lose the texture associated with grits. Our new process, however, has provided us with a corn grits product wherein the forming of an adhesive mass or cake is postponed several hours. This results in a product which retains the grits' texture for the longest of normal serving times for the product.

What a depressing triumph of science over taste.

JIM CRACK CORN

"The idiot who invented instant grits also thought of f rozen fried chicken, and they ought to lock him up before he tries to freeze-dry collards."

—

Lewis Grizzard

"I've got to move all this by end of the day," says Greg Johnsman, dodging around 50-pound sacks of food-grade yellow dent corn piled atop pallets in his storage barn at Geechie Boy Market & Mill on South Carolina's Edisto Island.

A heavyset man with impressive facial hair, the curlicue "Grits" logo on his T-shirt is dusted with meal. We're inspecting his collection of vintage milling and farm equipment. A Gibbs Machinery Company grits separator. A 1953 John Deere tractor. A seed cleaner picked up from an academic studying peas in Georgia. An early Meadows grits bolter, which has the serial number 382 hand-stenciled on its wooden casing. (Only 600 were built before the company shifted to metal housings in the 1920s.) Johnsman flips open the lid and points to a smudged signature. Neither of us can decipher the name but the pencil script reads "Edisto Island" underneath.

Edisto is my family's home ground. They have lived on this Lowcountry sea island for almost 325 years, through wars, pestilence, hurricanes, crop failure and real estate development. My father and brother are named for the place. My grandparents were born on adjacent farms. So were my great-grandparents. During several adolescent summer visits, Nana hauled me around to pay social calls in stuffy front parlors of plantation houses owned by distant cousins. Most mornings, some elderly female relative's lumpy grits were served at breakfast and less-than-politely declined by an obstinate child with no discernable table manners whatsoever. Every year or so, I go back to clean Spanish moss off headstones in the family cemetery plot, inhale the iodine scent of pluff mud at low tide and eat boiled peanuts. (If you're thinking, how can she like slimy peanuts but not slimy grits? Don't be a jackass.) Johnsman's operation is on the way, a few miles beyond the McKinley Washington Jr. Bridge on Highway 174.

While Johnsman's field hands unload collards from a flatbed truck parked in the cleaning shed, his wife Betsy fields orders from the storied Tavern on the Green in Manhattan's Central Park, and their 5-year-old son Victor drags me by the hand to show off his baby chicks keeping warm in a cardboard box. They are nearly the same sunny shade as freshly ground corn heaping up in the climate-controlled milling room.

"I've never bought a new mill," Johnsman shouts as the belt drive whirs on his mid-century separator. "Don't know what that's like. The old equipment turns at 600 rpm. The new equipment turns at 1,800 rpm." He sticks a scoop of grits under my nose. "The beauty of all this old equipment is that slow speed does not generate much heat and leaves the corn in its most natural state. If I mill corn right out of the field, that's cooking it. Here in the Deep South? This is the worse place in the world to mill with the humidity and everything."

Cracking corn is an ancient technique. (The 1840s folk song "Blue-Tail Fly" lyric "Jim crack corn" actually refers to rotgut corn whisky. What has it got to do with grits? Stick with me on this.) Before mechanized mills, there were metate or hand querns. The early Mayans boiled maize in an alkaline solution of water and lime, which softened the hull and made the kernels easier to grind, transforming it into a more nutritious substance known as nixtamal. The Native American word hominy defines the same process, but leads us into a sticky semantics side issue, so let's skip straight to what happened when colonial-era Americans introduced wind- and water-driven mills. George Washington's gristmill was a profitable aspect of plantation life at Mount Vernon. In 1790, the newly inaugurated U.S. Patent Office granted inventor George Evans Patent 3 for his automated milling technology. From there to Hyldon's Patent 3,526,512 is a matter of 177 years and several left turns in Southern breakfast history.

Greg Johnsman's separator falls somewhere in between on this timeline, before small mills became obsolete in rural Southern communities. When forced between his mill's bed and runner stones, the corn kernels are cracked, then sifted through screens as bran is skimmed off. The grind is adjusted depending on the orders Johnsman needs to fill. His grits are catching on beyond the "Belt." Naturally, Southern chefs like Sean Brock of Husk, Ashley Christensen of Poole's Diner, and Robert Stehling of Hominy Grill are faithful customers. But when the phone rings these days, it might be Christopher Kostow at Meadowood in Napa. April Bloomfield of the Spotted Pig in New York. Paul Kahan at Blackbird in Chicago.

"We can create all cornmeal or all chicken feed," he says. "But our business is making grits, so we have to find a common balance." He points to a crate of stitch-sealed paper sacks. "That's some Jimmy Red we just milled for Brock." He grabs up a bag of this rare kernel variety, which Slow Food recently added to its Ark of Taste heritage food catalog, and offers it to me.

At his roadside market, the two of us chug bottles of Cheerwine from the cooler and continue the history lesson. Above our heads hangs a battered wooden scoop.

"That looks insignificant, but it's one of the most special pieces I have," explains Johnsman. "A miller said to me: 'Son, this is the money.' Families brought in their corn and got the meal back. But the miller would take one scoop out of your bag and set it to the side. Then he would sell it to doctors and lawyers in town. So that's a tariff scoop. It's not a standard measurement, but it's how he made a living."

In the corner, behind piles of just-picked vegetables from the farm, sits a 1945 mill and separator he promised to put on display after buying it from a retired miller in Saluda, N.C. He points to an innocuous nail on one side below the meal screener.

"You see that nail?" he asks. "It took me two years to figure out what it was for. Someone prior to me found a shortcut. By adding that one nail was how he could hold a bag properly and improve the product process drastically.

"There's no miller store, no technical school; milling was just taught and passed on from whatever benefited each person," he continues. "So when I find these little nuances I kind of get to hold hands with a gentleman who came before me."

I examine an inscription Johnsman hand-lettered in black on the mill's wood casing: High Speed Chicken Feed.

"At the time, I thought it had to do with corn," he admits. "Someone had to tell me it's trucker slang for uppers."

JIMMY RED

When I was small
We had nothing at all
We used to eat Grits, for dinner
It was pain
Almost drive a man insane
What we could find for
To survive another day
But I said nah

—

RZA, "Grits"

"Yaller is for critters," recites Glenn Roberts.

In an outbuilding at Clemson's Coastal Research and Education Center (CREC), a few miles south of Charleston on the Savannah Highway and directly across from the seed vaults at the U.S. Vegetable Lab, we're looking at a kernel of Jimmy Red under a magnifying glass. If Johnsman is miller and farmer, then Roberts is miller and missionary. The founder of Anson Mills, this lanky Californian is an expert on antebellum identity crops. John Haulk, Bloody Butcher, White Eagle, Carolina Gourdseed White. Some have better pedigrees than a St. Cecilia Society debutante.

"If you grew up South of Broad in Charleston, you'd never eat anything but white grits," he says. Upcountry and farther along the frontier, he claims, common folk couldn't afford to be so picky about the color of their breakfast cereal. Roberts's second favorite hobby is hunting for feral plants. He drives an electric car. His mother was raised on Edisto during the Depression and learned her skillet skills from a Gullah nanny. Even though he grew up in California, the family still ate like Southerners.

"Mom had grits flown out to La Jolla," Roberts says. "My surfing buddies would come around and she would be making grits and greens for dinner."

Just in from the fields where late fall crops are still being tended, Dr. Brian Ward holds up the Jimmy Red kernel and identifies components for me: pericarp, endosperm, germ, tipcap. A horticultural specialist in charge of the Organic Research Farm, he wears khaki shorts, mud-scuffed work boots and a checked shirt bearing the university's bright orange tiger paw logo.

Remember I mentioned there was a connection between cheap booze and grits? The salvation of Jimmy Red may be tied to the illegal whiskey trade. Known formally as James Island Red, this auburn-hued corn was supposedly co-opted by Gullah moonshiners, who hid their stills in piney woods behind the fields they planted. True or not, it makes for a fine origin story. As Scott Blackwell of High Wire Distilling explains: "If you can get good grits out of a corn, you can make a good whiskey. There's a direct correlation between starch and sugar. And Jimmy Red's starch has character." Amateur seedsman Ted Chewning, who farms in the ACE Basin, acquired three precious ears from a friend who died before harvesting his last crop, insuring its tenuous existence. So far, Chewning has been able to trace the actual genesis to a farmer named Elmore Humphries, born in Screven, Ga., about 40 miles from the coast, in 1895. But that's where the trail stops.

"I have some of [Chewning's] original Jimmy Red in the vaults across the street," says Ward. "This kernel is from the more purified line. It took 10 years. We kept picking the best of the best plants in the field."

Roberts chimes in. "All maize was originally human sustenance. And it's non-persistent, so without human intervention, it does not survive. That's fairly unique because most of the early staple cereals were self-pollinating and self-replicating. Corn is different: It doesn't replicate, it will cross, it'll drift, it does everything you don't want a plant to do. If you hit on something that tastes really good you have to work hard to keep it the same."

Corn cultivation in the Lowcountry dates back to South Appalachian Mississippian mound culture. (That's 800-1600 A.D.) During the Antebellum era, plantations developed their own corn-provision systems with distinct cultivars — John Haulk, Henry Moore, Jimmy Red — that horticultural scientists like Ward consider the holy grail of Southern c orn flavor.

"Once you get a rare or culturally distinct seed," Roberts says, "the end goal is not to privatize it, but to get it back on people's tables." He turns to Ward. "Hey! Did you know Jimmy Red is selling for $18 a pound right now?"

Ward grins.

We move to a table where Ward has a dozen more oddball corn cultivars laid out. Roberts ticks off kernel shapes: "There's every degree of cross from flint to dent here." To understand the evolution of grits in the South, he asserts, it's crucial to know the morphologies and classes of corn, because some are more suitable than others for fresh grits.

"If you've ever tried to hand quern flint corn? It's the hardest substance produced by the plant kingdom," he explains. "And the reason you don't see grits in the North is because, as you move north, there's more and more flint class and you can't make fresh grits from flint corn. Dent is much easier to mill. Even so, coarse grits originally came into fashion because nobody wanted to have to pass it through a hand mill again and again."

Roberts and I take a spin around the fields where grape, indigo, sorghum and rice experiments are underway as Ward loads his truck with bins of heritage field-pea varietals being stored until the next planting season. CREC is based on a 325-acre farm that has been dedicated to agricultural research since the 1930s — after the sea island cotton industry finally collapsed, most Lowcountry farms shifted to vegetable "truck" farming; at its coastal facility, the University began developing disease-resistant tomatoes, okra, beans, melons and cabbage. Now, Ward's rare seed studies reflect the rising interest in preserving the earlier Lowcountry pantry.

"Want to know a good definition of old-fashioned grits and why we miss them?" Roberts asks. "There used to be signs on the side of the best toll mills that would say 'fresh grits.' And that meant new crop, fully robust corn with bright field flavor, still carrying nuances of sweet corn, as well as minerality or dairy or nuts. To keep chunks of the germ, where the flavor resides, along with the hard-starch endosperm, you have to mill to a big particle size instead of milling it all to powder."

So why did we ever shift away from something that at least sounds so delicious?

"Instant grits were easy," replies Roberts. "Coarse grits were the better way to get flavor out of a mill product but you give up speed: The cooking time is 90 minutes. Two hours are even better. Best? Soak it overnight, just let it ferment, expanding the flavor profile and nutrition of the corn. Then bring up the heat."

It's getting late and I'm hungry. Roberts walks me to my car. "Know what Native Americans call corn?" he asks.

I'm stumped.

"Mother."

DELICACY OR PRISON FOOD

Never call it "Hominy Grits"
Or you will give Charlestonians fits!
When it comes from the mill, it's "grist"
After you cook it well, I wist,
You serve "hominy"! Do not skimp,
Serve butter with it and lots of shrimp.

—

"Charleston Receipts" Junior League of Charleston, 1950

When Pat Conroy published "The Prince of Tides" in 1986, my parents copied out full paragraphs and left them taped to the refrigerator for each other to find. Late at night, I could hear them still snorting with laughter in our kitchen. Parts of chapter 11 were their absolute favorite, where Lila Wingo serves sweetbreads and coq au vin to her uncouth shrimper husband in a quixotic attempt to gain membership in the Colleton League via their snooty cookbook "containing the best recipes in the Lowcountry." As with the finest humor, it cuts close to the bone.

My mother was a self-taught cook. The only two books in her pantry were "Larousse Gastronomique" and "Charleston Receipts," which like Conroy's fictional version was compiled by Lowcountry ladies of a certain social standing. (My Nana's sister, Fannie Lee Anderson Seabrook, contributed a palmetto pickle recipe.) Similar to Glenn Roberts, I grew up eating Southern, although my parents relocated to New York before I was born. My mother's fried chicken, hot out of the pan or cold on a picnic, was food for the soul. Her spoonbread was lighter than cotton candy and her pan gravy smoother than velouté. She missed the soaking humidity of a Southern coastal summer, missed girlfriends who once danced the shag on weekends at Myrtle Beach, missed other people who sounded like her. It was she who encouraged the social calls with family who remain rooted in the Lowcountry.

I would be less crazy if she hadn't.

To be of a place but not from it has been the crux of a lifelong identity crisis. To lack the drawl yet still address collectives with "y'all." Belong to a clan 10 generations deep but live in a place where no one frankly gives a damn. Feel ambivalent on visits to the few relatives still occupying those big white houses on Edisto and South of Broad. Would it make me more authentically Southern if I did like that little white mound of food?

The Lowcountry's most ballyhooed dish is shrimp and grits. Unlike other regions in the Grits Belt, where country ham or livermush or red-eye gravy is its companion on the plate, the Carolina coast prefers shellfish for breakfast. (The height of shrimping season and the corn harvest overlap in the Lowcountry.) Always on the horizon this time of year, the commercial boats, rigging extended, nets dragging, a-sway on the tidal swell. But the tiny sweet shrimp that swarm in salt marsh creeks, rippling across the water's surface like a gust of wind, are most prized for this dish. The best way to catch them is to wade in with a cast net, bare feet sinking in the plumey sediment of decaying spartina grass.

The standard recipe in "Charleston Receipts" involves sautéing fresh shrimp in bacon grease with an onion and bell pepper. Stock from the pinched heads or shells and a little flour is added until the whole mess is slightly soupy. A dash of cayenne, a slug of Worcestershire. Then poured over hot grits. Comfort food for homesick parents.

Until recently, no one from Charleston would bother ordering homey shrimp and grits in a sit-down restaurant. Coinciding with the revival of fresh grits milling, however, Lowcountry chefs have put it on the menu for visitors "from off" who don't own a net or boat. Hominy Grill serves shrimp, mushrooms and bacon over cheese grits. Dixie Supply tops it with scallions and chicken gravy; a grossly sweet cube of cornbread squats on the bowl. I order yet another version at the Glass Onion drowning in mushroom gravy.

"You don't want it to look like prison food," says the waiter.

Or, I think, albino puke from a cardboard cylinder.

According to a spokesperson at The Quaker Oats Co., the South continues to be the largest per capita consumer of instant grits, and perhaps nowhere is that more evident than in St. George, home to the World Grits Festival. Every April since 1986, this town in Dorchester County, 53 miles upcountry from Charleston, has hosted a weekend celebration of grits eating and corn tossing. Almost 30,000 people attend. The festival highlight involves an inflatable kiddie pool brimming with viscous corn particles in a starch matrix. Contestants dive in, roll around and then weigh themselves. The winner has the most grits adhered.

Do not attempt this with Jimmy Red grits. While seedsmen like Ted Chewning and Dr. Brian Ward continue to propagate more, and millers like Greg Johnsman and Glenn Roberts stockpile it for certain lucky chefs, this pure line of hand-selected corn is still hard to come by.

"On the cob it's yellow," says Chewning, who spoke to me on the phone from his farm in Walterboro. "And only turns blood red when it dries down. We're guessing it was a moonshine corn because of the way it finishes after fermenting. Throughout the history of whiskey in America, people saved their seeds. But it's still a mystery. We all love a mystery."

One morning I drop by Husk, in downtown Charleston, where a plain pot of Jimmy Red grits awaits me. It's not South of Broad white or Critter yellow, but somewhere in between, flecked with telltale red bran. Cooked low and slow for hours, in equal parts water and whole milk, it has chewy density. Some weird alchemy between this milled corn and dairy imparts creamy, cheesy goodness. The corn's flavor isn't masked either. I eat a spoonful. Then another. And another.

I don't gag.

EPILOGUE

My mother didn't witness the fresh grits renaissance. She died up north unable to eat solid food in the summer of 1989. Her ashes rode in the trunk when we drove her back down South for the last time. One Christmas before she got sick, however, I gave her a kitchen apron, silk-screened with the wisecrack made famous by her favorite "Alice" sit-com character Flo. It read: "Kiss My Grits."

She wore it with pride.

— *Shane Mitchell is a travel and food writer with family roots in the South Carolina Lowcountry. Her 2017 story for The Bitter Southerner, "Who Owns Uncle Ben?," won the James Beard Foundation's MFK Fisher Distinguished Writing Award.*

First Published March 25, 2014

Go Tell It on the Mountain

◆◆◆

CHARLES MCNAIR

"Let freedom ring from Stone Mountain of Georgia."

—

The Rev. Martin Luther King, Aug 28, 1983

The last time he hiked to the top of Stone Mountain before embarking on a new life in South America, longtime Atlanta writer and novelist Charles McNair saw a ghost, had a dream and found a new, pure heart in the old mountain.

I had a dream.

The Georgia General Assembly funded a memorial for Martin Luther King Jr. and his top aides to be carved on Stone Mountain.

The lawmakers commissioned a bas-relief of MLK and John Lewis and Andy Young, this to be beveled into gray granite beside Jefferson Davis and Robert E. Lee and Stonewall Jackson. (A half-century ago, the Georgia General Assembly maneuvered to have that holy trinity of notable Confederates, along with their horses, carved onto Stone Mountain.)

At dream speed, hundreds of stonemasons dangled by rope down the side of the most famous ... and infamous ... pluton in the South. They lit the fuses on sticks of dynamite. They pounded chisels. They swung picks and fired up thermojet torches.

In no time, they sculpted a brand new Stone Mountain monument.

When the artisans stood back to admire their work, they beheld the great black generals of the Civil Rights Movement. They stood side-by-side with the great white generals of the Civil War.

Here stood a New Stone Mountain.

Many felt the fresh sculpture symbolically represented a start and a finish. Here, a single mountain face held the profiles of Southern men of greatest prominence at the start and the true finish of our century-old American Civil War.

A century of Civil War? It can certainly be viewed that way. The fighting between the blue and the gray ended in 1865, but the ongoing battle for equality under the law between black and the white lasted another 99 years, culminating with the 1965 signing of the Voting Rights Act.

So the new Stone Mountain stood for something. And, of course, the Georgia General Assembly wanted to make the attraction even better.

Lawmakers funded a new laser light show, twice as bright and dazzling. (Astronauts could see it from space.) They tripled the parking space to accommodate overflow crowds of visitors. Whites and blacks tailgated in racial harmony, knocking back Coca-Cola (with shots) and swapping recipes.

Stone Mountain Park sold MLK and Jeff Davis bobbleheads. Elvis sang over tinny loudspeakers, then James Brown took a turn. High school bands played Dixie and marched the five-mile path around the mountain. Then they marched around the mountain the other direction playing "We Shall Overcome."

Mass media fell in love. Social media fell in love too. Facebook buzzed like a billion bees. Twitter grew twitterpated.

Stone Mountain came to be an American version of the hajj, the trip to Mecca every able-bodied Muslim makes as an act of self-renewal. Every U.S. school kid grew up knowing he or she would visit Stone Mountain at least once in a lifetime.

All over the South, and then all over the world, lions lay down with lambs. Armies hammered swords into ploughshares.

People all just got along.

MIXLINGS & MONGRELS

I am happy to have this space in The Bitter Southerner to pull a thorn out of my 61-year-old heart.

My daddy was a bigot. He grew up at the knees of bigots, in the age of bigots. He raised six kids as a bigot. He went to his grave, I truly believe, an unreconstructed bigot.

Don't stop the presses. You'd be hard-pressed to find a white man raised in the Deep South in my father's day who wasn't a bigot ... or at least complicit in bigotry.

Look, we get a lot of revisionists nowadays. Southerners or their families glance back 50 years and claim they were better than that. These wishful thinkers hide behind the handy smokescreen of "To Kill a Mockingbird" and pretend they behaved a whole lot more like Atticus Finch than bigoted Bob Ewell.

The truth? Most white people of the day sat on porches and dipped snuff and shelled peas and didn't lift a finger while their yayhoo peers cracked the heads of blacks who had the audacity to think they ought to be able to vote or spend two bits at Woolworth's. Or get a drink from a water fountain, for God's sake.

My daddy was one of those people. In the living room and at the polls and in the coffee shop, Charles Cunningham McNair, whose name I carry, supported politicians and positions most willing to prevent "the mongrelization of the races," as I once heard him put it.

This meant, boiled down to its simplest terms, the blending of ethnicities that would inevitably follow integration and equal rights.

This Scots-English-Dutch-German-whatever-all-the-way-back-to-Africa mix ... who married a Scots-Irish-German-whatever-all-the-way-back-to-Africa mix ... and then created me and five other little McNair mixlings ... felt the sudden urgent need to avoid mongrelization.

THE VENERABLE VENABLES

One family vacation in the late 1960s, my daddy drove the family to Stone Mountain, east of Atlanta.

It was a sight anybody would want to see.

A sculpture of Confederate leaders spread out bigger than two football fields, the "largest high-relief sculpture in the world," as proudly claimed by Stone Mountain Park tourist literature. Jeff Davis and the generals in literal gray stood 19 titanic stories high. They loomed over the world, so gigantic that during the carving of the monument stone masons would scuttle inside a horse's mouth to keep out of Georgia thunderstorms.

The vacationing McNairs learned that the Stone Mountain carving began as a twinkle in the eye of a charter member of the United Daughters of the Confederacy (UDC). Inspired by her vision, in 1912 the venerable Venable family deeded the entire north face of the 300-million-year-old igneous core of a mountain once as tall as an Alp to the UDC for the purpose of creating a larger-than-life memorial.

The gift came with a 12-year deadline.

The original sculptor, Gutzon Borglum, received a commission in 1915, but World War I and money issues delayed work until 1923. After blasting rock off the north face for two years, Borglum ran into differences with his client, the Stone Mountain Monumental Association. He abandoned the project, escaping with his drawings and plans, leaving only Lee's head crowning from the rock. (The artist moved on to South Dakota, where he hacked Mount Rushmore from the granite of the Black Hills with more success.)

Another sculptor attempted the project.

Augustus Lukeman entirely overhauled the project's original design. (Borglum envisioned seven major figures accompanied by "an army of thousands," according to the park Web site.) Lukeman effaced Borglum's early work, toiled three years on a new carving of his own, then ran out of money. In 1928, the land reverted again to the Venable family. So after five years of physical work by two different sculptors, Stone Mountain displayed only Robert E. Lee's head — the new head carved by Lukeman and his team.

The solemn general's gray eyes stared balefully north for more than three decades.

In 1958, the Georgia General Assembly acquired Stone Mountain and the land around it. By this time, the Civil Rights Movement had gained real traction, and lawmakers who were playing defense against the school-integration mandates of Brown v. Board of Education (1954) and other legal and social attacks on segregation felt it incumbent upon themselves to memorialize the defiant rebel cause in various ways. They introduced the Confederate battle flag into the design of the official Georgia flag. They moved forward on a new Stone Mountain monument plan.

Nine world-famous sculptors offered ideas for the newest effort at a Confederate memorial.

The project's advisory committee settled on Walker Kirkland Hancock, a Massachusetts teacher and sculptor bearing the same last name as a Union general who outfought the Confederates at Gettysburg. (Hancock's men held the center during Pickett's Charge.) The Yankee sculptor Hancock achieved wartime fame in his own right as one of the Monuments Men of World War II, a group of soldiers responsible for rescuing looted art from the Nazis.

Hancock and his chief carving artist, Roy Faulkner, worked on the monument from 1964 to its finishing touches in 1972. Visitors to Stone Mountain Park today see their final vision of the memorial.

Politics aside, the Confederate monument remains a fantastically imagined and executed work of art — a world-class sculpture etched onto the most intractable of mediums, the stone heart of a mountain.

Conception to completion, it required seven decades.

THE MCNAIRS ON HOLIDAY

Stone Mountain would be only one of several stops on the Atlanta vacation of the McNair family.

We tramped through Six Flags Over Georgia on a 106-degree day, standing most of it in one endless line to board one lousy roller coaster. The soles of my brand-new Sunday shoes literally melted off on the blistering paved surfaces of the amusement park.

We went to a baseball game at Atlanta Stadium. Hank Aaron, that gifted black man, hit a home run for the Braves that night. My daddy drank beer, one of the very few times I ever saw him consume alcohol.

We discovered Krystal burgers. They cost a dime then. (An hour before, my outraged daddy marched the entire family out of a Howard Johnson's when he saw the hotel restaurant charged 65 cents for a peanut butter and jelly sandwich.)

Stone Mountain made no particular impression, though I remember its sheer enormity.

I knew all about the Confederates carved there too.

The Civil War played big in my house. One of my favorite boyhood books, "Generals In Gray," contained a picture and description of every Confederate general. (Just one lacked a photo.) As a child, I could quote you chapter and verse on

Bushrod and Stovepipe and Stonewall and That Devil Forrest. I could walk you through troop movements and blow-by-blow events of every major Civil War battle ... especially those won by Confederate soldiers.

We heard so much about the Civil War in my family because my daddy was one of those white southern people who simply couldn't stomach the thought that our great-grandfathers lost a war. Daddy came from people who couldn't stand the thought of losing anything.

Part of this attitude, surely, came genetically, a rebel DNA strand.

My people come from the Scots borderlands and Highlands. Folks from those places were "born fighting," as former Virginia U.S. Sen. Jim Webb put it in his book by that same name. The fiercely independent nature and the codes of manhood among Celtic emigrants to the South made them the perfect rebels — and damned fine soldiers — when war started.

People so bellicose would finally be subdued only by other Celtic warriors, men named Grant and Sheridan and Sherman, equally as fierce, but with bigger armies and more ammunition. Yankees also had a higher moral cause — the freeing of slaves — as an ultimate motivation.

After defeat, the Southerners who didn't have a thing to their names held the deepest grudges and longest memories. They fantasized a world like Tara to believe in, and they somehow made themselves and their sons and their grandsons — plus all those precious Daughters of the Confederacy — believe in a Lost Cause as noble and glorious as Eden before the fall.

Defeat left an indelible bitter taste and a persecution complex (warranted in ways). The grudge never faded.

I heard the historian Shelby Foote explain it once at a writer's conference in Birmingham.

In a Q&A session, a young man with a Yankee brogue took the mic. He asked the great historian how a Yankee could grow up in Pennsylvania feeling the great Civil War was history, a bygone event, yet move to Birmingham and hear people talk about the war "like it happened yesterday." The young man declared that he heard about the Civil War every single day of the year.

Shelby Foote gave this answer.

When I was a boy growing up in Mississippi, I had a number of playground fights.

I couldn't tell you much today about any of those fights I won.

But I can tell you every detail of the ones I lost.

A bumper sticker in the 1960s, a century after Lee's surrender at Appomattox, displayed a wild-eyed, white-bearded old Confederate with a rebel flag.

The caption: *Forget, hell!*

FIRE ON THE MOUNTAIN

Visitors to Stone Mountain Park see an amazing Confederate memorial. A certain history of the mountain, however, feels anything but monumental.

For many black people, for many years, Stone Mountain symbolized not Confederate glory, but something much darker.

In November 1915, a century ago, the following news story ran in The Atlanta Constitution, spelling and capitalizations as given:

Klan is established with impressiveness

Impressive services of the past week were those conducted on the night of Thanksgiving at the top of Stone Mountain.

The exercises were held by fifteen klansmen who gathered at the behest of their chieftain, W.J. Simmons, and marked the foundation of the invisible empire, Knights of the Ku Klux Klan.

The new secret organization is founded with a view to taking an active part in the betterment of mankind, according to the statement of its members who are known as klansmen, and the motto is "Silba Sed Anthar."

The rites incident to the founding of the order were most interesting and the occasion will be remembered long by the participants.

The Klan had swept back into vogue after "Birth of a Nation," the D.W. Griffith film that extolled the role of the terrorist organization in maintaining white power in Reconstruction. The 1915 lynching of a Jew, Leo Frank, by a white mob in Marietta, just 30 miles from Stone Mountain, further fueled Klan causes.

On top of Stone Mountain that Thanksgiving night, the Klan torched a rude cross. Two of the original Klan members took part in the ceremony. The event captured the public imagination so thoroughly that the Venable family granted the Klan ongoing rights to hold meetings at Stone Mountain any time they wished.

The Venables and the sculptor Gutzon Borglum — yes, the Mount Rushmore man — had Klan associations. Klan members filled the ranks of the original fund-raising organization for the Stone Mountain memorial. Even the federal government inadvertently helped, issuing in 1925 special half-dollar coins with Gens. Lee and Jackson on them.

(In fairness, the Klan had no presence at Stone Mountain when the state of Georgia condemned the Venable property and bought the site in 1958.)

The ugly history of Stone Mountain might have made it forever a place like Wounded Knee or Andersonville or any former slave plantation. It might have been a grim reminder of how America fails sometimes in the application of its first and finest value: "We hold these truths to be self-evident, that all men are created equal, that they are endowed by their Creator with certain unalienable Rights, that among these are Life, Liberty and the pursuit of Happiness."

But something happened.

And something is still happening.

NOTHING IS SKIN DEEP IN THE SOUTH

My daddy drove our big white station wagon around Dothan sporting a GEORGE WALLACE FOR GOVERNOR bumper sticker. When Wallace's term limits as governor ended and his wife Lurleen Burns Wallace ran as his proxy (she won), my daddy cut up two Wallace stickers, rearranged and inverted letters, and fashioned a new bumper sticker: MA WALLACE.

My daddy pulled our station wagon off two-lane Highway 231 late one night. He walked me and my two little brothers down a grassy slope and through a sedge field to a Klan rally.

Three crosses burned in that field that night. Whatever else, the Klan could put on a show. What young mind could ever forget the powerful images of white spectral figures with gaping eyeholes and cans of gasoline setting Jesus's own cross on fire? At age 10 or so, I could easily have swallowed the bait of bigotry. Hook, line and sinker.

So many others did. I'm still not entirely sure why I didn't.

So, fellow Southerners, here's the ugly thorn. Look at it. Right at it. Here's my father, the bigot. His brown eyes gleam in the light of burning crosses. His three impressionable sons stand in his giant flickering shadow.

But now let me give my daddy's story a little twist.

Just about everything in the South gets more complicated if you scratch the surface. Nothing is skin deep here.

Life fell apart at age 12 for my daddy.

One afternoon when the kids got in from school, his mother dropped dead in the front room of their house in Troy. The McNair children watched their father leaning over her already lifeless body. He rubbed a wrist, crying, "Mary! Mary!"

Before the shock subsided, the aftershock.

The father remarried, to a woman who worked very hard, if you believe the family tales, at driving away all four children of the first wife.

My dad found himself a runaway at age 15, sleeping in the straw of a barn full of dairy cows. At age 17, with his own father's help, my daddy enlisted in the Air Force.

After two tours in the Philippines, he came home to Alabama, met my mom just as she was graduating from Troy State Teachers College, and started a family.

He tried his hand at carpentry. He built one house and sold it. He built another, and it sold too. Soon, he bought land tracts and sold lots to other builders until he made back his investment. He turned a profit on the remaining subdivision parcels, building and selling houses as McNair Construction Company.

He quickly learned that to make real money he needed to stop driving nails and start driving deals.

So who built the houses?

He hired two permanent crew members. His white foreman, Gene, had thumbs on both hands somehow flattened out into the shape of big toes by years of hammer blows. Gene could read house plans, and Gene could use a framing square, the two essentials for building a three-bedroom, one-car-garage McNair home. Gene showed up for work in a blue Chevrolet pickup every day precisely at 10 minutes to 7 a.m., rain or shine.

The second crew member, Willie Rogers, hired on at age 18. Willie rode to work in the mornings and rode home from work in the evenings in the cab of my daddy's truck for more than 30 years. Every model Chevrolet we ever owned smelled like my daddy's Tampa Nugget cigars and the eye-watering body odor of Willie Rogers.

Willie was black. A nigger, back then.

Like John Henry, Willie was a steel-driving man, only the steel he drove came out of a cloth belt full of 16-penny nails. Willie could outwork any human being I ever saw … and I know this as an eyewitness.

Every summer from age 10 to age 25, I crewed with my daddy, desperately attempting to earn his approval and to amount to something in those stern brown eyes.

I flung dirt from a hundred miles of ditches with Willie Rogers. I hammered a half-million nails into floors and decking and two-by-fours and trim alongside Willie Rogers. I hoisted hundreds of wheelbarrows full of heavy wet concrete with Willie Rogers.

No matter how fast I dug or nailed or rolled or did anything else, I would look up, pouring sweat in the brutal Alabama summers, to find Willie already moving on to the next job. He just seemed superhuman.

He was my daddy's man.

In 30 years, Willie might have voluntarily spoken 30 words to my daddy. Daddy did the talking. Willie did the working.

Every Friday at 4 p.m., my daddy signed a paycheck for Gene, one for Willie, one for me and my brothers, if they happened to be working. By Friday midnight, Willie had generally blown his week's pay. So he showed up nearly every Saturday afternoon, in a car driven by some weekend buddy, reeking of Hai Karate and malt liquor, to make a draw from his next paycheck.

This went on for decades, a circadian rhythm of work and reward, loan and repayment.

When Willie got cut up in fights, my daddy paid the hospital bill. When Willie got thrown into jail for eyeballing — serving as a lookout for two thieves taking apart a Coke machine — daddy posted bail. When Willie got slapped with a paternity suit (Judge: Willie, is this your child? Willie: I reckon) my daddy made sure the child support reached little Freddie Rogers.

My daddy began to buy land as he grew prosperous selling homes. He quilted together 4,000 acres, most of it planted in loblolly and slash pines ... most of the pines planted by Willie Rogers.

On the coldest days of the year, Willie would climb out of daddy's green pickup before the sun rose, step out on the frozen ground, then start the back-breaking work of hand-planting pine seedlings, one by one. Except for a break at lunch — always a can of Vienna sausages, a box of soda crackers, a honey bun and a Coke — Willie worked till the sun went down.

He worked can to can't, as the saying went. I know, because I planted pine seedlings too, trailing far behind on my rows.

Willie worked weekends when he needed to make good on his deeper debts. He worked holidays.

You could call the relationship of my daddy and Willie Rogers a metaphor ... or a stereotype. How many white men for three centuries rose to prosperity by exploiting black muscle and sweat? How often had the nests of white children been feathered ... with black feathers?

So ... here's the old bigot at the construction site barking orders to his hired man. Here's the old bigot riding for miles to reach fields where young pines wait to be put in the ground. Here's the old bigot frowning in court beside Willie as a judge dispenses justice.

And here is where things get really complicated.

THE COLOR OF DUST

After I had gone away to school and begun to unmoor, with years of pain, from the Honor Thy Father commandment, I got a phone call.

I lived in Birmingham then, a college graduate after 12 years (not a typo) as an undergrad, paying my own way. I had a job with the telephone company, making decent money at last. My writing had begun to show up here and there. I finally felt like a grown man ... and my own man at that.

On the phone, news. Willie Rogers had passed away. Some kind of cancer. He suffered. His funeral was coming up.

I drove to Dothan. My daddy and I dressed in Sunday suits. We went to the church where Willie Rogers rested in a coffin lined with pink satin.

The cancer had reduced this superhuman working man to the size and physiognomy of a black baby-doll. My daddy wouldn't look into the open coffin.

We stood in the back of a drafty church, about as basic as a house of worship could be. It surprised us that so many people came to see Willie off. He appeared such a loner to us white folks. That day, we were the loners, the only two white people in the church.

When time came to say nice things in remembrance of Willie's life, a few folks spoke up. I cleared my throat. My daddy always had an unholy fear of public speaking. He let me do the talking.

I told how Willie helped me understand that all people are equal. Except I didn't really feel equal at all. He could outwork me at anything I ever tried.

We returned to daddy's truck after the funeral, passing up the graveside service.

We settled into the cab. My daddy, the old bigot, took a deep breath. He wanted to say something to me.

Then he began to weep.

And finally, he began to sob like I never heard any human being sob before or after in all my life.

Every time daddy tried to catch his breath, he uncontrollably blurted out a hysterical, heartbreaking sound that has only one meaning in this world.

I realized at that moment how deeply my daddy loved Willie Rogers. Loved him.

Here lay the great duality of Southern whites. The bitter South.

My daddy could somehow hold an enduring, deep, honest love for a black man at a personal level. But somehow, for whatever damning reason, he could never let that benevolence extend one black soul further ... never mind to embrace an entire race of people.

I will go to my own grave bewildered at this mystery.

How could my daddy love a black man, but see nothing worth respecting in Black Man? Was it a willful refusal? Was it just an act all along, a way to appear recalcitrant, like granite? (Who knows what's really in a man's heart?) Was it simply a human flaw, a prejudice like each and every one of us displays in some way, at some time, to some person or group, consciously or not?

Every one of us.

My daddy passed away 10 years ago. In the end, he turned to the same dust as Willie Rogers.

The same color dust.

IN TIME, ALL THINGS ERODE

Unique to Stone Mountain and a tiny surrounding geographical area, a rare yellow daisy blooms in fall each year. The lemony petals surround a black center. A Yellow Daisy Festival commemorates the blossoming.

Like that daisy, surprising communities and subdivisions have sprouted on the land around Stone Mountain since the 1960s.

The towns around Stone Mountain have filled — surprise! — not with bigots or Klansmen, but with middle-class black families, many of them professionals who fight the traffic down U.S. 78 each day into downtown Atlanta. They report to jobs in law offices and corporations and utility companies and hospitals and state and federal buildings. They wear jackets and ties and Anne Taylor suits. Many don't even know ... or else don't care ... that Stone Mountain once symbolized hate for people their color.

A great many ethnic communities cluster close by, too. A well-attended, fantastically ornate Hindu temple stands in nearby Lilburn. Clarkston knows celebrity as home to the famous Fugees soccer team, a collection of immigrants and lost boys and people rescued from trouble spots all over the world.

These blended people, a United Nations of suburbia, go see Stone Mountain. They visit the park in droves, heedless of Confederate memorials or laser light shows glorifying ancient U.S. history. They bike and jog and hike miles of trails and paddle waterways, simply enjoying the natural beauty of the outcrop. Many regular visitors no doubt wonder who the heck those gray men carved on the mountain might be.

The white misdeeds at Stone Mountain, like the mass of mountain that once soared 20,000 feet high around it, flake away with time.

YOU ARE THE MOUNTAIN

Stone Mountain now has a new champion.

"By the lottery of birth," as she puts it, Shannon Byrne grew up in Stone Mountain, Ga. She graduated from high school there, attended the University of Georgia just a stone's throw away. With an English degree in hand, she bought a one-way plane ticket to New York City 10 days before the start of the new millennium. She arrived with $400 and a suitcase.

Irrepressible, charming, pretty, energetic, Byrne landed a job as a book publicist. After a few years, she returned to the Atlanta area to do publicity as a freelancer. She represents Michael Connelly, the best-selling crime novelist.

On her return, Byrne rediscovered the mountain she'd left behind.

It hurt that the place she enjoyed so much, a one-of-a-kind park filled with woods and water and wonders, had been stigmatized by racial issues.

Byrne set out to right an old wrong, to bring redemption to an old sinner. Her personal, one-woman mission to reinvent the image of Stone Mountain seems as monumental as the old rock itself.

I Am The Mountain, Byrne's Web site, celebrates the diverse community she finds thriving on the trails and summit of the mountain. She blogs, photographs, interviews, provokes, challenges. A visit to the IATM site leaves one questioning anything and everything ever assumed about Stone Mountain.

"This website humbly attempts to illustrate freedom ringing at long last and to celebrate all of the new faces that are reclaiming the mountain," Byrne posts on the homepage of her site.

"I moved back to Atlanta from New York, and found myself climbing Stone Mountain an awful lot for exercise and head-and-heart-clearing goodness," she says. "What amazed me most upon my return to the mountain itself after years away were the people I began meeting there from all over the world.

"It wasn't this diverse when I was younger, so I was absolutely moved by what appeared to be the mountain's transformation from the infamous 20th-century rebirth place of the Ku Klux Klan, 100 years ago, into such a stunning ethnic mosaic of so many new faces."

In the summer of 2014 alone, Byrne met, photographed and captured the stories of mountain hikers from Ethiopia, Mexico, Colombia, Somalia, India, Pakistan, Nepal, Guatemala, Vietnam, Cambodia, Israel, Saudi Arabia, Haiti, Afghanistan, Iran, France, Japan, Guyana, Venezuela, Kenya, Moldova, Kazakhstan, Bangladesh, England and South Sudan. She interviewed refugees from Myanmar who had been living for years at a camp in Thailand. She met a young man of Mexican and Palestinian descent. (Byrne herself is half Mexican, one quarter Irish, one quarter English.)

One afternoon, I hiked the mountain with Byrne. No one we met on the way up or down could resist her.

We talked with Muslim girls from Africa, a Chinese family, a Russian woman who shared her lunch and stretched out a hammock so travelers could rest briefly and listen as she read verses from a Bible. Hikers passed in turbans. Hikers went by on artificial limbs, undaunted by the steep 1.3-mile hike to a summit more than 800 feet above the surrounding Georgia landscape.

Swarms of kids darted past. Women in burkas descended from the heights. A photographer lugging a tripod and long lens chuffed by. An extreme fitness freak, running, passed us going up. Twice.

On top, seated on a wind-and-rain polished rock, a pair of teenage lovers shot selfies, snuggled close.

All those people. All those stories. Red and yellow. Black and white. All are precious in Shannon Byrne's sight.

Mark my words: This is not your father's Stone Mountain. Not anymore.

KEEP WATCH FOR THE SPECTER

For a quarter-century, every winter and summer solstice when I wasn't traveling, I climbed to the top of Stone Mountain.

Something compelled me to get to that high place to see the shortest and longest days of the year. I witnessed maybe 30 solstice sunsets.

I loved to see Atlanta in the west that time of day, a city on fire once again, 150 years after Sherman.

A watersmooth mountain path to the crest always felt holy to me, the climb a meditation. The mountain seemed a righteous way to start a new year ... or a new life.

On Jan. 28, 2015, my 61st birthday, I relocated to Bogota, Colombia. I love a special woman here.

My last trip to the summit, the winter solstice before Christmas 2014, only five weeks before my move to a Deeper South, something happened on the mountain.

I had a dream. A waking dream.

I had made it to the top and found a smooth rock for a seat near one of those strange waterholes that miraculously hatch fleets of little shrimp when conditions get just right. (Shrimp live on top of Stone Mountain. Don't tell me it's not a wondrous place.)

The solstice sun fell. It goes down very fast when you watch from the mountain. You have a keen sense of the earth spinning on its maypole at 1,000 miles per hour. Dark rushes in, a star or two flares in a purple sky. The lights of

Atlanta and its merrily mixed suburbs twinkle like a man-made Milky Way.

Sweat as you might on the arduous path going up, the summit always feels chilly. This day, I nearly froze to death. The Arctic wind blew all the way from Canada, nothing to stop it before Stone Mountain.

Still, I lingered after sundown, savoring the solitude and the beauty of it all. Knowing how way leads on to way, I felt this might be a last goodbye. I might never make it to the top of Stone Mountain again. I might not ever live in the South again.

At last, stiff with exertion and cold, I struggled to my feet. I set off down the smooth stone path toward my car, then my home.

Not a hundred yards down the trail, I spied a figure climbing toward me in the gloaming, passing in and out of view among the bonsai pines of the mountainside.

It stopped me in my tracks.

I give you my Bible oath that the approaching silhouette looked exactly like my daddy.

The walk was distinct. Daddy had a stroke toward the end, and his right arm dangled. He favored his right leg when he stepped. He never quit trying to move on his own, without any help.

The whippoorwills called, out in the woods. I heard a train, that low harmonica. Those same sounds filled childhood dusks on Parish Street in Dothan, when we sat on the porch and listened to my daddy tell about growing up and how he learned things.

I waited, still as could be, for the figure to near.

It never did. No one ever came up the path. I waited

10 minutes, rooted to that one spot. It got so cold I could no longer feel my feet.

Finally, I eased on down Stone Mountain. I kept vigilant every step for ... what? A ghost? Apparition? *Doppelgänger?*

It happened months ago. But I've been thinking that maybe the old Confederate, God bless him, still walks the trail up there on Stone Mountain.

Somebody please let me know if you run into him.

Stone Mountain is a forgiving place now. A place where redemption feels possible, real. Right.

Shannon Byrne, if you see that old man, tell him I miss him and love him so much ... and I forgive him, no matter what.

And ask him to forgive me, for what I had to write.

— Charles McNair is the author of the novels "Land o' Goshen," "Pickett's Charge," and "The Epicureans," which was serialized in The Bitter Southerner.

First Published June 10, 2014

The Last of the Alabama Gang

♦♦♦

CLAY SKIPPER

I've been hearing things at night in the big old house.
It ain't just the pistols and the frogs and trains.
It's a rumbling sound, rising like red-clay clouds,
From the ghosts of the Alabama Gang.

—

"Dirt Track," Lee Bains III & the Glory Fires, 2014

Red Farmer was the oldest of a group of Hueytown boys who dominated auto racing in the '60s and '70s. He's still racing the dirt tracks at age 82, and he can still outrun most things. Except maybe time.

In the noon sun of a bitterly cold January day at the Talladega Short Track, an 82-year-old race car driver worries about time.

His name is Red Farmer, and he holds a stopwatch in his chapped palm. His hands are black and oily with grease, and dirt is underneath his fingernails. He sits just beyond the track's catch fence, close enough that the skidding cars on the other side leave a coat of red-clay dust on his glasses. He watches intently as his friend Luke Hoffner takes his race car — "Ol' Yeller," Red calls her — on the first round of her Friday "hot laps," practice runs for Saturday's qualifiers. Track officials are recording times for the drivers, but Red likes to track the seconds himself. He knows each one matters.

It smells like gasoline, and each time the cars come around the 1/3-mile dirt oval, it sounds like a plane taking off. Red leans forward in the golf cart — his "huntin' buggy" — that he drives around the track's complex, his mouth slightly agape beneath his white goatee. Years spent driving fast, trying to outrun the clock, have left their marks all over him. There are deep creases at the corners of his eyes, and grooves in the skin lining the back of his neck. Three of the fingers on his left hand are missing.

I'd heard stories about Red Farmer, the octogenarian race car driver, the oldest member of the legendary "Alabama Gang," which dominated racing in the 1960s and '70s. But I wanted to see for myself, so I came here to Talladega's lesser known racetrack, one made of dirt, for its most popular event, the Ice Bowl, which has run every January for the past twenty-four years.

Red's won at Daytona, and he's won at the other, much bigger Talladega, and he's already been inducted into the

International Motor Sports Hall of Fame even though he hasn't been retired for the requisite five years, because he might never retire. He's been here for all 24 Ice Bowls, though five years ago, he couldn't race because pneumonia hospitalized him for a few days at the end of December. He still came anyway, because what's a little cold weather to a 77-year-old who just got over pneumonia?

Red's parked on the backstretch, and each time Luke completes a lap, Red presses the stopwatch so hard his whole hand shakes, like someone is timing him time Luke. Luke runs three or four laps and then exits the track and heads back to Red's hauler in the pits. Red backs his buggy up and as he's turning around, I jump on the back. When he guns it, I almost fall off.

"I don't wait for nobody," Red shouts over the roar of the next round of cars coming onto the track. A few more seconds pass and he takes off down the hill, a longtime race car driver speeding off in his camo-upholstered huntin' buggy.

"I ain't got time," he says.

GRANDMA'S TIRES

The Talladega Short Track is located on Speedway Boulevard, not far off I-20's exit 173 for Eastaboga, Ala., and past two gas stations that sell fireworks, too. It's marked with a big sign — "Talladega Short Track, Dirt Trackin' Southern Style" — and a right turn will put you on the gravel path to the track, a long line of pickup trucks parked alongside. The immense grandstands of the Talladega Superspeedway are about a mile down the road. Here, at a short track made of dirt, NASCAR's corporate presence hovers always but rarely touches. They are two racetracks on the same road and in different worlds, a body disconnected from its own beating heart.

The men and boys at Talladega Short Track are named John Parker and Jeff Jones and Kyle Smith and come from towns like Piney Woods, Ala., and Shelbyville, Tenn., and Jasper, Ga. They drive cars sponsored by Choice Concrete Walls or Oliver Trucking or Brewster Builders. They're all over the dirty pits, red with clay and frozen to the bone on this early January weekend. They arc dipspit into Styrofoam cups or hold cigarettes between fingers so black with grease that you wonder if maybe their hands will never be clean again, if they've ever been clean before. They buy coffee and corndogs and Rolaids — only $1! — from ladies named Debbie and Loretta who work concessions and who will put chili and cheese on anything and probably won't charge you for it either. They'll give it to you and they'll say, "Thank you, honey," or, "Have a nice day, baby," and you'll think of your mom even if you haven't seen her in a long time. They wear hoodies that say "There's only 3 speeds: fast, really fast, and oh shit!" or "You dump it, we pump it." There's camo and Carhartt everywhere. They wear overalls and boots and work pants because when they race the cars they built, they are going to crash them, and when they do, they'll rebuild them too, and then race them again. They are all the teenage driver from Clanton, Ala., who found a race official before the Ice Bowl started and asked, "What time is this going to be over? I borrowed the tires from Grammy's car."

And they are all Red Farmer too, a man who won Daytona in 1971 and Talladega in 1984 and 1988, but who likes racing over here, where dirt and grease get in your fingernails and skin, and where "you gotta drive with the seat of your pants, the feel of the car ... you got your ass. That's it." It's more fun without the radios, or the spotters or the rearview mirrors they have down the way. Because sometimes you can't look too far forward, and you don't want to see what's behind you either. You just want to keep running straight ahead. And sometimes all you have is your grandma's tires, or your 82-year-old ass.

CRAWLING FROM THE WRECKAGE

Today is Friday, and tomorrow will bring the qualifying races for the 2015 Ice Bowl, but Red's not yet sure if he's going to race or not.

"I don't know what the hell I'm gonna do tomorrow," he says, standing by his two race cars in the pits, in the shadow of a scoreboard that's falling apart but is still in use, anyway. "I'm worried about today."

It would be the start of yet another racing season, 67 years after he ran his first race at the Opa Locka Speedway in Florida. It wasn't so much a "speedway" as an abandoned airport. The drivers would run down one runway, drive through the grass and dirt to another, and run back.

It was there in Florida where he started working with a young man named Bobby Allison, and not long after, Red, Bobby and Bobby's brother Donnie came north to race in Alabama. They set out all over the Southeast — first from a one-bedroom apartment they all shared, and later from a garage in Hueytown — running cars wherever they could, working on each other's race cars and towing them wherever they went, sharing rooms and meals, sometimes racing two races in one day, or three races in three cities in three days.

The Alabama Gang, they were called, because they were boys who lived and worked in Alabama, and because of the prize money they always took. They drove their way onto the NASCAR circuit and they won there, too. Red won three consecutive NASCAR Late Model Division championships from 1969 to 1971. Bobby's son Davey started racing, and he became part of the Gang, and so did another Hueytown driver named Neil Bonnett. In February of 1988 Bobby Allison won the Daytona 500. Davey finished right behind him. Neil Bonnett finished fourth. Two and a half months later, Red won at Talladega Superspeedway.

The Alabama Gang was on top of the racing world with no way of knowing it was all about to start falling apart, before disintegrating completely.

Bobby Allison doesn't remember edging his son at Daytona. In June 1988, he crashed in the first lap of the Miller High Life 500. He survived, but he would never race again and he would never get his full memory of 1988 back. Donnie quit racing not long after. He had crashed years earlier — in 1981 — and could never get back to being the driver he was before, the driver Bobby and Red had once raced with. Davey kept racing and in 1992, he won Daytona just like his dad before him. The following year, he was flying a helicopter to Talladega to watch Neil Bonnett's son. It crashed and he died. Farmer was in the helicopter with him, but survived.

After the crash, Farmer and Bonnett were the only ones left of the original members. In 1994, Bonnett returned to the Daytona 500, which he would run without the Alabama

Gang, and without the father and son he once finished just behind. He ran into a wall in practice. He died nearly six years to the day after the Alabama Gang took three of Daytona's top four spots.

Red can't ever forget the year his friend Bobby, now 77, won't ever remember — 1988, the year Red won at Talladega and the year the Alabama Gang was still whole and alive, before they started dying off. They'd all walked away from crashes in their career but Red kept walking away when the others stopped. People started talking about a curse. Red had been Davey's crew chief in the Busch series, and also like a dad and hero, too. Davey even named his dog Old Red Farmer. Red made it out of the helicopter wreckage Davey couldn't. He was put back together, but loss leaves holes doctors can't find, and though Red didn't die, something did. He never raced at Talladega Superspeedway again.

Now, on a cold afternoon in January, he tries to decide whether to drive a race car or not, standing in the shadow of that racetrack and in the shadow of something else too. Like any shadow, it gets longer as the sun sets, until it settles over everything. It follows Red, reminding him that no matter how many times you go round and round the dirt oval, no matter how fast you run it, all drivers still end up at the same spot. He learned something watching racetracks and race cars harm or kill his friends: Race car drivers don't die from driving but from hitting something so sudden and so final they could never hope to run through it. You don't die from going too fast. You die when you stop.

RACING WITH JESUS

Though he's unsure about what he'll do tomorrow, Red's going to run in the second round of hot laps today.

Everyone wants to talk about how old he is, and how crazy it is that he's still racing at his age. Maybe he likes that, because as long as people keep asking when he's going to stop, he doesn't have to answer other questions — from others or within himself — about the loss and suffering he's endured and that's robbed him of so much more than the 82 years have. And yet, for everything the racetrack has taken, it has given something too. The curse of so many drivers isn't that they're destined to die in their race cars, but that they won't stop until they do. Racing is the salve for some soul-burning flame they can't ever put out, that only driving fast can quench. Red's been racing and working on cars since he was a young man — a boy even — since before there were meet-and-greets or lights or private jets or fancy haulers, and the racetrack's been a home, a refuge through all of the pain. Racing is how he lives, and it's how the rest of the Alabama Gang would've kept on living too.

Red has two race cars: the yellow and red GRT Model that Luke was racing earlier — it runs a Chevy motor — and a white Ford Rocket with a smaller Ford motor that he will run. Both cars run Hoosier Tires, and while many spoilers around the track have messages like "Jesus" or "To My Love" or "Thanks Dad" or "Roll Tide," Red's GRT says, simply, "Hoosier Daddy." Really, the cars are nothing more than a few pieces of flimsy metal strapped over a roll cage, a steering wheel, a thin, uncomfortable seat and a motor that makes it all go very, very fast. There's a Driver's Prayer sticker pasted inside the car and a Racing With Jesus sticker just outside, because death hangs heavy at a racetrack, and, regardless of your religion, sometimes a roll cage isn't enough.

Red was once 6'1" and 210 — he played football for the Army when he served in the early 1950s — but he's smaller now. He's trim and with a slight hunch, gravity slowly exerting its force over time, pulling him closer to the dirt he races on. He has the trace of a hobble, but when he swings himself through the driver's side window of a race car, he's remarkably lithe. He has only five whole fingers and two thumbs to hold the steering wheel, having chopped part of three fingers on his left hand off in his airboat propeller in the 1960s, before packing up the boat, driving it back to shore, hopping in his car, driving to the hospital and then racing later that weekend. Because Red Farmer is always moving, doing something: racing or working on a race car, hunting or fishing.

"You hunt? You fish? What do you do?" he asks me at one point.

Uhh, I write?

"That's boring as hell," he says.

Red fires up his engine and when he does, the whole car shudders violently, and the sparse grass growing up out of the dirt bends in the opposite direction, like it's trying to run away. He faces forward in his Tasmanian Devil helmet and the car settles into a steady, pulsing rumble, both comforting and ominous, like there's something deep inside that wants out. Red gets ready to head out onto a freezing racetrack in a dying sun and do the same thing he's always done, still unsure if he'll race tomorrow or not, because he's worried about today.

No spotters. No rearview mirrors.

After he's done, he'll come back to the pits, and as the sky turns to black and his crew puts the cars up for the night, a man will approach Red with a flier for a race in April, asking if maybe he'd want to run in that race.

"April?" Red will ask. "Hell, I don't even buy green bananas anymore."

ONCE THEY WERE HEROES

After Red leaves the racetrack for the night, his presence lingers in two pictures that hang in the press box at the Talladega Short Track. They're on a dark wood plaque that says, "Race of Champions, May 4, 1990. A Night to Remember." Here on a Friday night nearly 25 years ago, Red Farmer outran The Intimidator himself, Dale Earnhardt. Earnhardt won an IROC race down the road at Talladega Superspeedway the very next night, before winning the Winston 500 on Sunday, too.

The short track's press box sits inside a red cinderblock square at the back of the bleachers. The carpet is red and stained, and the room is wood-paneled. There's something musty and vaguely crotchety about it. If it were a person, it'd probably hate the sound of those damned race cars on the track below. An empty fridge and a square, clunky television with hand dials on the front sit against the right wall. An open storage room has fiberglass insulation poking out of the walls. There are blue-cushioned chairs in a row at the front of the room, facing out the square windows and onto the track below. In the night outside, the Ice Bowl's smallest division is running its heat race, and the car next to Red's in the pits is out there racing, the black one with both a green number and a "For Sale" sign taped to it. The barriers on the inside of the track — between the cars and the infield — are white, and a small fence above them is covered with sponsoring businesses: Riteway Bail Bonding ("Get Out of Jail Almost Free"), O'Reilly Auto Parts and Oxford Love Stuff, an adult store that once supplied a box of promotional gift bags that included some unlabeled pills in a plastic bag. The glass windows and cinderblock structure dull the buzz of the cars' motors, but the sound hovers constantly.

This buzz, which gave the track its nickname, the Hornet's Nest, has been the background noise to Rita Donahoo's life. She's 53 and has been coming to this track since 1983 and says she's done "every job here," or, as PA announcer Eddie Davis puts it: "She pretty much runs this shit." She has dirty blond shoulder-length hair that's big and curly. She wears a blue and yellow Sunoco-branded jacket over a sweatshirt and blue jeans. Rita grew up among brothers and her grandfather used to take them to the track, but told her, "This is not for girls." She came anyway, and in 1983 a driver named Mike asked her to score for him, since the track did — and still does — use hand scorers. That was their first date. Now they're married and their son Mikey is a flagman here, and she likes that family feel. Kids 9 or younger still get in free, and entire families can spend a night at the track for just $20. The kids sit right along the catch fence and pick a favorite driver for the night. They look through the metal wire and they see young drivers from nearby towns or states, and that's a distance they can measure. At least three people will tell me that dirt racing is "grassroots racing," where anyone with a car can run — even if that car's for sale.

Rita points out the two cars running in the current heat, one of which looks like it just left a demolition derby, and one that runs up front and looks faster than it is because it's shiny and bright and looks like a real race car.

"It can look like that without the fancy lettering job or it can look like this car here in second place with that really neat job," she says, before bringing attention back to the beat-up looking car. "This guy, he may not run out front, but he can still get out there and have fun with them."

That's not the case with NASCAR, where big money rules. Bobby, Donnie, and Red ran at a time where the gulf between a clay short track and an asphalt speedway wasn't so wide, when NASCAR was still a sport grounded in the Southern dirt it came from. Rita remembers the days when NASCAR drivers would make the short drive down the road from the Superspeedway to come here. Her son would throw a football with their sons.

"They would run with our late model drivers," she says. "But then it became to where these guys were as big and, you know, insurance property. You didn't want them to get hurt."

Soon, the heats will be over, and the 200 or so people scattered throughout the bleachers will gather up their blankets and their space heaters and head back to their cars. They'll be covered in red clay. It'll be on their boots and jeans and in their eyes and in their mouths. They'll get it in their cars when they drive out past the sign that says "drive safely" on the way out but not on the way in; and they'll track it in their houses when they get home, because clay sticks to you in a way that asphalt can't.

"They're not of the people anymore," Rita continues.

A phone rings somewhere in the press box.

"But when they were to where you could meet these people and see 'em, they were real humans" — the phone rings loudly again and Rita seems to notice this time — "and they were heroes."

She stands up and walks to the other side of the room.

"Then they became celebrities," she says over her shoulder before picking up the phone.

Red Farmer never left. He still races here, and though he may be older, he's still a damn good driver. But he can't race forever, and soon the only Red Farmer at the Talladega Short Track will be the one in the pictures hanging on the back wall. There's one of him shaking Earnhardt's hand and one of him solo, posing with the checkered flag and his winning trophy. Earnhardt's dead, and only Red remains, except, in both photos, he's completely washed out, the details of the picture fading with a quarter-century of time. There is his car, and the track, and the people in the stands, but inside the outline of Red's body, the only distinguishing marks are the barely visible lines of his fire suit. He's a glowing, white ghost, and there's a blank space where his face should be.

YOU CAN REBUILD A CAR

Saturday morning is beautiful and blue and windy. American flags flap in a wind that smells like America too, reeking of cigarettes and gasoline. Red's worried about his race car, because he's always worried about his race car, because that's easier than worrying about other things. Because when a race car wrecks, you can build it back into what it once was, and make it faster, more efficient. Because there's always another race for a car.

His tires keep wearing out. The turns are tighter on dirt because the track is smaller (the straightaways are only 400 feet vs. about 4,000 at the Superspeedway). Cars whip around them, drifting or sliding in a way that's more violent than it is on asphalt. The cars screech and the tires get hot, which helps them connect with the track, until, eventually, they get torn up. The key is finding a tire that'll get hot without wearing out, and then hoping the caution flag doesn't come out, because when a car slows down, its tires cool off, messing up its rhythm. A fast-going race car never wants to stop.

When Red decides on the tires to use, the crew cut grids in them so they can better grip the track. Then they put them on and get the cars ready to race: checking the oil, monitoring tire pressure, refueling. The cars are clean because Red has them wiped down at the end of the day. The crew clean off the red clay and the oily grease, and it gets on them, their hands and clothes getting dirtier and blacker.

Red always works with them, a driver and his crew. But today, he's on the same side, preparing the car for someone else, because after his time trials and his preparation, he has decided he can't race, and the reason is a reminder that mortality is unflinching and unsentimental: His stomach is acting up, and he worries the bumps of a dirt track might make him shit his pants, making dirty the car he likes to keep unsoiled.

"I ain't cleanin' the seat," his crew chief says.

Red's grandson, Lee Burdett, is going to run in his place, as he has before. All Red can do is watch and hope that the tires run well and run fast and hook up to the track, and that when they do, they don't give up before the race is over.

Maybe one day Lee will replace Red in this car permanently, or some other driver will, giving new life to an old car. Today, it was his stomach. Five years ago it was pneumonia. Humans aren't race cars. They get old. They can't be wiped clean or put back together or rebuilt. They can't be made better or faster, and with each race that passes Red by, the old man he's become grows a little farther from the young man he used to be.

YEAR 1,000,000

Red sits in the grandstand named after him (just as the bigger Talladega's backstretch is now named "The Alabama Gang Superstretch"), wearing a tan, hooded Carhartt jacket that says "Red Farmer Racing" across the back and waiting for his cars to come onto the track and run as fast as they can, trying to outrun the stopwatch that tracks every second gone. When Lee finally crests the hill, trailing red clay in his wake, the PA system announces his arrival, booming excitedly. "...and celebrating his one millionth year of racing, the 97 car of Red Farmer!"

Red Farmer isn't in the car. He's sitting in the Red Farmer Grandstand, across the track from the press box where a fading picture of him hangs in the shadows of a dark room, watching younger men do what he's done for so long. He'll sit and watch intently as the cars go around and around and around, until the race is over and they stop and they turn their engines off, and all that's left is a cloud of dust and a deafening silence in the wake of so much noise.

— Clay Skipper was based in Mississippi when he penned this story for The Bitter Southerner. He is now on the staff of GQ in New York City.

First Published June 17, 2014

The Dirt Underneath

◆◆◆

CHUCK REECE

Will Harris began trying to return his family farm to pre-industrial methods just because it felt like the right thing to do. Twenty years after he began this process, his White Oak Pastures has become America's grandest experiment in the de-industrialization of agriculture.

"Industrial agriculture is forced by its very character to treat the soil itself as a 'raw material,' which it proceeds to 'use up.'"

—

Wendell Berry, "Agricultural Solutions for Agricultural Problems," 1978

I am standing in the middle of Pine Street in downtown Bluffton, Ga., with no worry of being run over. What little traffic there is in Bluffton moves slowly. Next to me stands a demonstrative man. He is pointing.

First, he points north, straight up Pine Street.

"OK, there is a strip of land that starts about 10 miles that way," he begins and then turns and points southwest, "and goes about 15 miles that way. It is anywhere from a few yards wide to maybe a mile wide, probably not quite a mile. It is really good land because it's where the Appalachian Mountains went subterranean.

"Highway 27 right here, the old one, was built on the Indian trail that ran along that crest."

He points east. "Everything on that side of the road drains to the Flint River."

Now west.

"On this side of the road, it goes to the Chattahoochee River. That's important because this soil is an uneroded mountain soil. This is uneroded because there's nowhere for it to run."

The pointing man is a farmer named Will Harris.

He teaches me that we are standing on a strip of the same good land that drew huge numbers of native North Americans to a place called Kolomoki, about seven miles southwest of Bluffton, 1,600 years ago.

Kolomoki back then was the most populous area north of Mexico, like New York City is today.

You can still visit Kolomoki, but it's now known as Kolomoki Indian Mounds State Park. In the early spring, it is mostly devoid of people, save a few curious tourists and the one state park ranger staffing the visitor's center. Nothing remains of the old civilization except the ceremonial mounds, which archaeologists tell us were used in the religious practices of the Swift Creek and Weeden Island people.

Kolomoki is quieter than a church on Saturday night. It hasn't been a hopping town in more than a millennium. But the grasses and trees around the mounds are brilliantly green, because underneath it is that good land, fertile topsoil black and rich in organic matter on a bed of the red clay that defines the American South.

In this heavily agricultural part of southwestern Georgia, much of the cropland is now freshly plowed for spring planting, shining bright red in the sun. What that color tells you is there is little to no organic matter left to serve as topsoil. This is the result of our country's move to industrialized agricultural. After decades of being treated with chemical fertilizers, these red-clay fields with which we so strongly identify can now produce food only with the aid of chemical fertilizers.

But here we are, Will and I, right in the middle of a strip of land once so naturally rich that an entire civilization called Kolomoki rose up on it.

Can such land be redeemed? Yes, absolutely. But it takes time and great effort.

REBUILDING THE ORGANISM

"The form of the farm must answer to the farmer's feeling for the place, its creatures, and its work. It is a never-ending effort of fitting together many diverse things... It must have within its limits the completeness of an organism or an ecosystem, or of any other good work of art."

—

Wendell Berry, "Renewing Husbandry," 2004

Will Harris' 1,250-acre White Oak Pastures has been in his family since 1866, when his great-grandfather, James Everett Harris, came to Bluffton. Under the direction of James' grandson, Will Bell Harris, the current Will's father, it became a modern cattle farm after World War II, when traditional methods of farming began giving way to industrial methods.

Then, about 20 years ago, Will Harris turned back the clock. He slowly began to exchange the methods of large agribusiness corporations for something different. He stepped back two generations to the methods of his great-grandfather, to a way of farming that depends on the keen eyes of the cowboy traveling endlessly through the pastures, vigilant for small changes, determining when it's time to move a herd from one pasture to another, to give the land a rest.

Today, you can pick up a handful of earth from anywhere on Harris' 1,250 acres and not see red. Here, there is topsoil. It feels friendly in your hand. It smells so good you almost want to eat it. The grasses and legumes that spring up from it feed great herds of cattle, hogs, goats, sheep, rabbits, chickens, ducks, guineas, geese and turkeys.

White Oak Pastures has turned itself into one of the largest — if not the largest — pasture-raised livestock operation in the entire nation. It is the only pasture-raised livestock farm in the nation with its own separate slaughterhouses for hooved animals and for poultry.

In the process of making the transition back to the old ways, Will Harris accidentally became something of a celebrity among foodies. A recent story in The New York Times said, "If the Southern organic crowd were made up of teenage fan girls, he would be their Justin Bieber."

One of Harris' daughters had to tell him who Justin Bieber was, and when he was told, he didn't much care. But let's not be too hard on the Times, because it's difficult for any journalist who visits White Oak Pastures (including this one) to resist the lure of writing about Will Harris the character instead of about Will Harris' farm. He wears a ridiculously sweat-stained Stetson Open Road, the same model his daddy (and LBJ) always wore, except Will trains his into a narrow-in-the-front, wide-in-the-back profile. That's his look. He travels the pastures in a pickup truck with a short-barreled rifle lying on the console. He is a born storyteller of the highest order, and his deep South Georgia accent sounds, by his own admission, "like Foghorn Leghorn." Will Harris the character is irresistible.

But the better story, the story that actually raises big questions about the future of the South, is the one about the ecosystem Harris has built — which happens to include more than 100 people with some pretty great tales to tell.

On any given day, White Oak Pastures is home to eight acres of vegetables, an entire pasture devoted to composting, and at least 72,000 chickens being raised for meat, 9,000 egg-laying chickens, 3,000 ducks, 2,000 guineas, 2,500 geese, 1,000 sheep, 1,000 goats, 700 cows, 100 hogs, 100 rabbits and 200 turkeys (although the turkey population will swell to about 7,000 this month with the arrival of young heritage-breed poults that will be raised for slaughter during the holiday season).

More importantly, the White Oak "organism," as Harris calls the whole shebang, includes 110 employees — a crazy quilt of South Georgia country boys who make good livings as meat cutters and young folks from all over the world bearing degrees from places like Cornell and Harvard. What's weird is that all of them, regardless of background, talk about a common purpose:

They want to work on a farm where they can experiment with their theories about how to feed the world without raping its land.

Nofarminthenationsoconfoundsourconventionalwisdom: that it is impossible on a large scale to return to the methods of old, where nothing is wasted and farm animals express instinctive behavior in the environments nature designed them for. Judged against the revenue of giant agribusiness corporations, White Oak's entire operation amounts to pocket change. And to be sure, there is no consensus among those who study the world's food supply about how much this kind of farming can contribute to feeding a global population — now more than 7 billion people and still growing.

But White Oak Pastures' scale has become big enough to make people take notice at a very interesting time, when a growing number of consumers are becoming concerned not only about the hormones and chemicals in the meat they eat, but also the welfare of the animals that become our food.

White Oak Pastures is, at this moment, America's grandest experiment in the de-industrialization of agriculture. And to understand that story, you have to understand the importance of the dirt underneath.

THE ROAD TO DAMASCUS

"Soil ecosystems are threatened by the progressive loss of organic material as farmers abandon organic for chemical fertilizers and offer the land less fallow, or resting, time."

—

the United Nations Population Information Network,
"Population and Land Degradation," 1995

Will Harris stands knee-deep in the greenness of one of his pastures, telling me how his father, Will Bell Harris, moved the farm into the industrial age.

"Daddy took over the farm after World War II, in 1946," he says. "He said they had a farmer meeting in Bluffton. salesman from the ammonium-nitrate company held a fish fry at the peanut mill. They invited all the farmers. My daddy went."

As corporate America began converting the nation's new manufacturing capacity to peacetime uses after the war, ammonium nitrate became cheap and abundant.

"The salesman had 100-pound bags of ammonium nitrate, and they'd dip five or 10 pounds into a brown paper bag and give a bag to every farmer. He said, 'When you get home, take it out there in your yard or your pasture and just make a pile, a straight line or a circle, write your name or whatever you want to do. Put some water on it and don't look at it for three days."

Will Bell Harris did just that.

"Daddy came back three days later, and the grass was like this high," Harris says, holding a hand at about waist level of his six-foot, 60-year-old frame. "It was black green instead of pale green and Daddy said, 'Shit! I want the whole farm to look like that.' And so he did. Every year from 1946 until about 2003, the time I quit using it, we put ammonium nitrate on every acre every year."

Every year, they used 200 to 400 pounds of nitrogen fertilizers per acre.

Harris' father continued into the modern age of industrial agriculture, introducing the use of so-called "subtherapeutic antibiotics" and hormone implants. He began feeding the cattle cheap and abundant corn, even though cattle are not designed by nature to eat it. But corn made for tasty, fattier meat at the dawn of fast-food restaurants, which demanded megatons of cheap ground beef.

When Will Harris graduated from the University of Georgia's College of Agriculture in 1976, his father told him he had to work elsewhere before he could return to the farm. He took a job with Gold Kist, which was gobbled up by Pilgrim's Pride Corp. in 2007, one of the world's largest meat producers. He rose to become a regional manager in Gold Kist's Agriservices Division, overseeing the operations of the company's cotton gins, peanut-buying points, fertilizer-blending facilities and grain elevators in parts of Georgia, Alabama and Florida.

Will continued to work on the family farm, some days putting in eight hours at his job and then another eight on the farm. In 1995, Will Bell Harris' declining health pushed the farm's leadership role to his son. And in the beginning, Will held firmly to the industrial model of his father.

"There were a lot of excesses in that production system, and it's kind of interesting: Those excesses were things I really enjoyed," he says. He remembers the way he used to view the advent of new "treatments" designed to make his cattle grow faster.

"Man, they've got some new shit that you can give cows, that you can inject your cows with? Bring it on! They say give them 2 cc's every 100 days, that's what the label says. But you can really give them 3 cc's every 50 days. And my calves weighed 20 pounds more at weaning per calf. On 700 and something calves at a dollar and something a pound, that's great. And then they've got some other stuff they're coming out with, and you ain't supposed to give it straight into the brain, but ..."

He pauses.

"I loved excesses."

But as the end of 1995 rolled around, he found himself feeling differently.

"I started getting a little bit disgusted about it," he says. "Probably, if I had played by the rules, I wouldn't have gotten disgusted by it."

Will Harris is not a church-going man, but that was the beginning of a long, slow conversion experience. He knew he had to orient his farm in a different direction, although he did not fully understand what to do to make it happen.

"It was a long way from being something I could articulate," he says. "The first thing we did was give up hormonal implants, subtherapeutic antibiotics and feeding them corn. I gave it up and liked it, and I was thinking, this is good, I like this better."

I ask if it caused the farm to lose money.

"It caused me to make less money," he answers. "Less was OK. But we were still making money."

Then, in 2003, he took a much bigger leap: He stopped putting chemical fertilizers on White Oak's pastures.

"Giving up chemical fertilizers caused me to start losing money," he says. "Chemical fertilizers are good stuff, and it takes a long time to get off them."

More than once as we roam the pastures of White Oak, Harris makes it clear he believes chemical fertilizers are to a farmer as heroin is to a junkie.

"When I first gave up chemical fertilizers, my pastures looked like shit."

But he persisted, and two or three years later, the farm's bottom line turned black again. So did the soil in his pastures. The percentage of organic matter in his farm's soil today, Harris says, is about 10 times higher than the soil of nearby conventional farms. Two years after that, he introduced sheep, heeding what farmers have known for centuries: that raising different species on a single farm benefits both the land and the animals.

He later began reading the books of Wendell Berry, a Kentucky farmer who is also one of the South's most prolific writers. Berry, now 80 years old, has published 28 books of poetry and 15 works of fiction, but people in the food world are most familiar with Berry's non-fiction. He writes passionately, frequently and authoritatively about farming, especially in his 1977 book "The Unsettling of America: Culture and Agriculture." "Unsettling" is a polemic about the unintended consequences of industrial agriculture, in which Berry essentially argues that the health of people and the health of the land are inseparable — and that industrial ag practices constitute a fundamental threat to the natural symbiosis between people and land.

"I conceive a strip-miner to be a model exploiter, and as a model nurturer I take the old-fashioned idea or ideal of a farmer. The exploiter is a specialist, an expert; the nurturer is not. The standard of the exploiter is efficiency; the standard of the nurturer is care. The exploiter's is money, profit; the nurturer's goal is health — his land's health, his own, his family's, his community's, his country's. Whereas the exploiter asks of a piece of land only how much and how quickly it can be made to produce, the nurturer asks a question that is much more complex and difficult: What is its carrying capacity?"

With the farm changing around him as a result of his earlier decisions, larger questions began gnawing at Harris. He had rid the farm of all the artificial inputs he could control. His animals roamed the pastures freely, foraging instinctively, as nature designed them. But there was one aspect of his herds' welfare he could not control: the way in which they were slaughtered.

Will Harris could no longer stomach the idea of loading calves he had raised onto double-decker trucks, in which they'd travel hundreds of miles way, with neither food, water nor rest, to slaughterhouses run by one of the four big agribusiness companies — Tyson, Cargill, JBS and National Beef — which process 80 percent of America's beef.

"When I majored in animal science at the University of Georgia from '73 to '76, good animal welfare meant you don't intentionally inflict pain and discomfort on the animal," he says. "That's like saying good parenting means locking your children in a closet at 72 degrees and leaving the light on."

So he did something crazy, something no conventional cattle farmer would do these days. He hired the renowned animal-welfare expert Temple Grandin to design a slaughterhouse to be built on his own farm. Then he borrowed $7.5 million against his family's land and built it. It went into operation in 2008. Today, no animal at White Oak Pastures ever sets foot on concrete until a few seconds before its slaughter.

"When I went and borrowed all that money, we were hemorrhaging money for about four or five years, but I was never 30 minutes late paying anybody. We finally caught traction and it started making a little more, then a little more. Now it's not a really profitable business, but it's a good enough business."

In 2010, Harris introduced chickens to the farm and added a second slaughterhouse for poultry. Since then, he's added seven more species to the farm: hogs, goats, rabbits, chickens, ducks, guineas, geese and turkeys. Today, White Oak Pastures is a paragon of biodiversity. Its gardens turn out a wide variety of organic vegetables, its beehives produce wildflower honey, and logs sprout fresh mushrooms. All its animals, with the lone exception of breeding rabbits (a fact that still annoys the heck out of Harris), roam its pastures freely.

Harris' slow journey on the Road to Damascus, by now almost 20 years in the making, may have been a spiritual awakening, but it did not turn him into a religious man. As he often notes when talking about the history of the Harris family, "We are profane people. We were pretty rough compared to our neighbors — irreverent, profane, talk too loud, drink too much, cheat to win."

But Harris has become more watchful, more deeply conscious of the consequences of his actions, and perhaps even a little prayerful. In the Pavilion restaurant at White Oak Pastures, where a chef prepares meals, which are about as "farm-to-table" as you could possibly get, for visitors and employees every day, an unusual prayer is painted above the window into the kitchen:

"We pray for plenty of good hard work to do, and the strength to do it." It's a prayer he remembers from childhood.

"I get that prayer," he says. "Most of the exposure I've had to different faiths, I don't get most of it. But I think if you are given plenty of good, hard work to do and you're given the strength to do it, everything else is pretty much OK."

That night, over a supper of chicken quesadillas with Will and his wife Von, he says the same little prayer. Then, to maintain a proper balance of the sacred and the profane, he pours us glasses of Pappy Van Winkle, the world's most coveted bourbon.

"Julian (Van Winkle) is a friend of mine," Will says. Stardom in the food world evidently does have its privileges.

FLIES, BURRITOS & LASAGNAS

"The factory farm, rather than serving the farm family and the local community, is an economic siphon, sucking value out of the local landscape and the local community into distant bank accounts."

—

Wendell Berry, "Stupidity in Concentration," 2002

One of the first people I meet at White Oak Pastures is Jean Turn, the farm's financial controller. In our first brief chat, she says something I will hear repeatedly in later conversations with White Oak folks: that she thinks of the entire farm — the pastures, the gardens, the animals and the people — as a single organism.

I figured I'd hear that kind of talk from Harris himself, but I didn't expect it from an accountant.

But Turn is right. To witness the 110 people of White Oak Pastures do their daily work is to see them function as a single unit with a singular goal: that nothing goes to waste, that nothing is ever, to use Wendell Berry's words, "used up."

Lori Moshman, 24, splits her time between sprouting

the plants that will later mature in the farm's eight-acre (and growing) vegetable operation and making sure, in her way, that nothing is wasted. She grew up in Brooklyn, N.Y., earned a degree in entomology at Cornell University, and then moved to Bluffton to work at White Oak.

"I told my mom that I wanted to work on a farm after I graduated, and that kind of started a long series of very painful conversations with her," Moshman says. "It's just something that for my parents, who both grew up in New York and have never lived anywhere other than New York, it's just something that they can't imagine at all and didn't understand. Their impression of farming is I'm going to shovel shit all day. It took awhile to convince them that it's really a lot more than that. They've since come around quite a bit."

Her parents now visit the farm twice a year, she says, and they're impressed.

They should be. When Moshman came South at age 21, she started as an apprentice in White Oak's gardens.

"Since then," she says, "I have become greenhouse manager and black soldier fly manager."

If you're wondering why a farm needs a manager of black soldier flies, you have to understand that these little insects, which look like all-black fireflies and are abundant in South Georgia, produce larvae that are among nature's most efficient recyclers. They eat meat waste and turn it into food that chickens absolutely love.

Two old silos, which stored corn for the cattle before Harris went old-school on everyone, have been turned into breeding chambers for thousands of black soldier flies. Moshman runs this operation with a dude from Spain named Alfredo Llecha, who has long, wispy, salt-and-pepper hair and looks more than a little like Geddy Lee, the bass player from Rush. Moshman and Llecha harvest the larvae of the black soldier flies in the chambers.

"We have two goals for the larvae," Moshman explains. "One is to eat up all of the organic waste that comes out of our two slaughterhouses on the farm so that it reduces the amount of waste handling that we have to do, and then to produce a protein- and fat-rich feed source that can be used to supplement (the diet of) our pastured poultry."

The whole process is natural genius. Large sheets of burlap are laid on the ground and covered in meat waste from the slaughterhouses. The burlap is then folded over on itself and then rolled into what the White Oak folks jokingly call "burritos." Each burrito is then laid on a squirming mass of a few thousand black soldier fly larvae.

The result is food for the chickens of White Oak Pastures.

"It's not on a farmwide scale yet," Moshman says. "We're still pretty small, but we've made some really great advancements since the time I've been here. Right now we've pretty much figured out the system that we're going to use, so it's just a matter of scaling up and getting the labor to do that."

The large-scale compost heaps at White Oak are called "lasagnas." They are giant alternating layers of meat waste, peanut shells and other carbonaceous material, distributed evenly across one large pasture. Each lasagna matures for two years, and the resulting compost is spread on the other pastures.

The chicken feed that Moshman and Llecha produce from the wastes of the red-meat slaughterhouse is consumed by flocks that are under the care of a Savannah native named Frankie Darsey.

"I have this memory of my dad with baby cardinals in his shirt in Savannah, and we wanted to touch them, and he wouldn't let us touch them," Darsey, 42, tells me one day out behind the poultry slaughterhouse. "He was like, 'Well, I'm going to put them back and hopefully they'll live because we haven't touched them.' I didn't know what that meant, but I think what that instilled in me is that everything has the right to live, and what we think is best for an animal might not be the best thing for an animal so we have to think like an animal, and I'm glad I kept that memory."

To talk so deeply about caring for chickens directly behind a building in which they are slaughtered seems a bit ironic, but only if you look at it through the lens of industrial agriculture. Almost all the chickens we eat these days are raised in closed "broiler houses." A typical broiler house of the current design is about 36,000 square feet, and it will house 36,000 chickens — only about a square foot per animal. They live brief six-week lives to reach a slaughter weight of about five pounds, growing that fast only through the aid of chemicals. A 2009 report from the University of Georgia Cooperative Extension Service said the "typical" flock of 25,000 chickens in Georgia broiler houses has a 3 percent mortality rate. Many of the remaining chickens suffer from blindness caused by ammonia fumes rising from all the feces that piles up during the growing cycle.

The website fusion.net, a joint venture of Univision and the Disney/ABC Television Network, sent shockwaves through the broiler industry with its recent six-part documentary, "Cock Fight," which not only gave the public a rare look at conditions inside broiler houses but also documented that "71 percent of U.S. farmers who only grow chickens live at or below the poverty line."

By contrast, here is what the lifecycle of a White Oak Pastures chicken looks like:

The first thing to note is that the cycle lasts 12 instead of six weeks. That's how long it takes a chicken to mature to slaughter weight without artificial assistance.

It starts with one-day-old Freedom Ranger chickens. Darsey tells me the Freedom Ranger is only about four hybrid steps away from a heritage-breed, or purebred, chicken. The chickens that populate most conventional chicken farms are about 36 hybrid steps up from heritage breeds, he says.

The chickens spend the first two to four weeks of their lives, depending on the weather, in a brood house, until they are old enough for the outdoors. Then they are loaded by hand into plastic laundry baskets and from there placed by hand into an open trailer filled with peanut shells. The trailer is hitched to a tractor and pulled out into one of the pastures. Out on the pastures are movable coops; they're hauled to a new patches of ground after the chickens pick each one clean. The chickens get gently herded into a newly cleaned coop, filled with food and water. They spend only one night confined to the well-ventilated coop, "long enough for the homing mechanism to kick in," Harris says.

From there on out, the chickens spend the eight to 10 remaining weeks wandering all over the pastures by day and returning to their coops by night, not by force but by instinct.

"For us," Harris says, "good animal welfare means they can express instinctive behavior."

At slaughter time, the chickens are gathered into coops and brought a few at a time to the poultry slaughterhouse. The animals are hung two or three at a time by their feet on a metal apparatus, and a slaughterhouse worker touches the neck of each one with an electrified knife that stuns the bird senseless. You can see its muscles relax and its feathers go limp. Immediately, the knife is drawn swiftly across their throats. They bleed out into a system that captures the blood from both slaughterhouses and recycles it for other purposes around the farm.

Watching an abattoir at work is not for the faint of heart, but the butchers of White Oak work with great care, not only in how swiftly they dispatch the animals but also in the steps they take to ensure the cleanliness of the meat they deliver to supermarkets from Pennsylvania all the way down to Florida.

If your diet is dictated in any way by concerns about animal welfare, it doesn't get much better than this. The chickens spend most of their time in the sunshine, pecking around the farm, until it's time for them to become your dinner. And when that time comes, they never know what hit them.

Mary Bruce, 25, brought her chemistry degree all the way to Georgia from the suburbs of Detroit to go to work at White Oak Pastures.

"I was a vegetarian until I came to this place," she tells me one day as we watch the soldier-fly larvae do their work. She's seen vegetarians visit the farm who wind up eating meat before they leave. "They're like, 'We still don't eat a lot of meat but we'll have it from you because we know you're doing the most respectful thing to the animal.'

Where else do you find someone who actually respects the death of the animal? And then what happens afterwards ... it's profound."

She starts talking about how cowhides become rugs or wallets sold in the farm store. "And then the beef fat makes terrible compost, so we started making soaps, chapsticks, candles."

The fat, by the way, is also turned into biodiesel to help power the farm's vehicles.

"It's just a big loop where nothing gets wasted," she says. Mary points at Will, who is standing nearby, and says, " just think about how hard he works to just make sure that every piece of that animal has a use."

BIG CITY, TURN ME LOOSE

"Perhaps the most urgent task for all of us who want to eat well and to keep eating is to encourage farm-raised children to take up farming."

—

Wendell Berry, "Conservationist and Agrarian," 2002

Will Harris treated Jenni Harris, who is now 28 years old and White Oak's director of marketing, the same way his father treated him. He told both Jenni and her younger sister Jodi Harris Benoit, who today is manager of farm events, that they had to work elsewhere for at least a year before he would let them come back.

"It was a great rule," Jenni tells me in a conference room in the headquarters office of White Oak Pastures. "He said, 'It is my intention to create an opportunity for you but not an obligation. If you work here it will be because you chose it, not because I pressured you into it. It won't be your only option, it will be an option.'"

So Jenni, after finishing her marketing degree at Valdosta State University, moved 228 miles north to Atlanta.

"I knew I wanted to work with White Oak Pastures," she says. "I didn't know at what capacity and I also didn't know what strengths I had and what I could bring to the farm, where I would be most valuable."

So she took at job at Buckhead Beef, a food purveyor to restaurants in Atlanta and customer of White Oak Pastures, and set about learning exactly what was required to bring the meat of her family farm to chef's tables in the big cities of the South.

"Everybody can make money based on the value that they bring," she says. "We are farmers. Our value is producing it and selling it. Chefs transform raw stuff to cooked stuff and present it to the consumer, who eats it and enjoys it. That's the chef's value. What value does the distributor bring? It's in always having product, keeping it cold, covered and sealed and delivering it on time. That's a really hard thing to do with consistency."

She loved the work. She learned a lot.

"Then 365 days from the day that I took the job, my ass was back home," she says. "I am not an Atlanta person. I enjoyed it for its conveniences, but I have never felt more lost in my life. Who would have ever thought that the little girl that grew up with 16 people in her graduating class, that always wanted to do something different and express a part of her that was not able to be expressed the first 23 years of her life, would move to Atlanta and still feel lost as shit?"

When Jenni talks about the "part of her that was not able to be expressed," she is referring to the fact that she is a lesbian. Growing up that way is not easy in a place such as Clay County, Ga.

"I had a hard time watching things falling into place for everybody else and things being so wrong for me," she says. By going to Atlanta she wanted to figure that out. But she could not resist the call of the farm.

"I was ready to be back," she says. "I had told my dad, 'I'm coming. You can find something for me to do. It might be working on the kill floor, it might be mopping floors, I don't give a shit. I'm coming home.' I got home and my dad said, 'You've got a marketing degree, Would you like to be the marketing manager?'"

By the time she got home three years ago, White Oak was already successful selling its grass-fed beef and pasture-raised chickens wholesale to supermarket chains such as Whole Foods and Publix. So Jenni set to work on expanding two other markets, both of have higher profit margins than the wholesale biz: selling to chefs and directly to consumers over the Web. Going to market that way makes a lot of sense for an operation the size of White Oak.

"When you talk about keeping stuff in stock and always available and keeping it consistent, those are two of the big complaints that people have when working with local farmers," Jenni says. White Oak is now big enough to deliver a steady stream of whole chickens, eggs and ground beef to supermarkets, but the same is not true for the other outputs of the farm. The farm is now very large and its red-meat slaughterhouse runs at full capacity five days a week, but that's only 35 animals a day, maximum. Thus, you will not always be able to find a White Oak-grown ribeye steak every time you walk into a Whole Foods.

So Jenni is doing what smart marketers do, turning her company's disadvantages into advantages.

"What separates us from the commodity market is that it is inconsistent," she says. "That makes it beautiful — because it's not always available." What she's doing, really, is making White Oak's marketing strategy a reflection of the seasonal nature of the farm itself.

The natural seasonality and variation in weight of the farm's products do not matter to shoppers who order from whiteoakpastures.com. They are able to buy whatever is available, when it is available, thus making them ideal retail customers. Jenni's other ideal customer is a chef — but only a certain kind of chef.

"One of the first questions I ask a chef who wants to work with White Oak Pastures is, 'Do you celebrate inconsistency?' And if they say, 'Not really,' then I go ahead and say, 'We might not be for you. If you order a case of lip-on ribeyes, they're not all going to weigh eight pounds. That's our spec, but they're not all going to weigh exactly eight. And they're not all going to look alike. Is that OK with you?' If they say, 'Yes, that's great. I'm a chef and I'm trained and I can handle the curveball you throw,' that's who we want to work with."

Jenni might not have been comfortable during her year in Atlanta, but these days, she probably has more relationships with more of the South's great chefs than even the most ravenous foodies. She will not speak publicly about which Southern chefs are her favorites, but she will allow that she has frequent e-mail exchanges with one of her favorites along these lines:

"Hey I've got a lot of lamb testicles this week. You want to try 'em?"

"Absolutely. Send me 20 pounds."

During her first year back at White Oak, Jenni wrestled with another problem, one unrelated to the marketing puzzles she was solving. While living in Atlanta, she had fallen for a woman named Amber Reece. She wanted to get Reece to move from Atlanta to the farm, but before that could happen, she had to come out to her parents.

She nearly worried herself to death before she told her mother, Von.

"Talk about being stressed, the night I told her, I broke down in tears," Jenni says. "She was convinced I was dying of cancer by the time I finally got it out of my mouth. At that point, she had knelt down beside me and was like, 'Whatever it is, we'll deal with it. Are you in trouble? Are you sick?' She was just freaking out, frantic. And I was like, 'No, I'm not any of those things. I'm gay.' She was like, 'OK, that's fine. You want some macaroni?'"

Her father's reaction was not much different, she says: "OK. Want to go out and ride around the pasture?"

He did, however, give her advice that she took.

"He was fiercely proud of me," she says. "It did not make a difference to him, but he wanted to make sure that I was absolutely sure that this was what I wanted because there were consequences of it. He wanted to be certain that, if it was what I truly wanted, I was going to handle the negative comments. That was straight fatherly advice, but I was sure. I was 100 percent sure at that point. I mean, I was 25. I had found the person that I wanted to spend the rest of my life with. I told him that and he said, 'That's good. If you want me to, I'll run an ad in the Early County News and we'll tell every motherfucker around. And if they've got any questions or comments we'll put my cell phone in the ad.' He's had my back since day one."

She remained worried about her coworkers at White Oak.

"I was stressed out about moving Amber here," she says. "It's Southern culture to the core."

I ask how this has worked out.

"They fucking like Amber better than they do me," Jenni says, smiling. "I mean everybody. I have had not one single negative thing said about me or my relationship. Not only do they not say negative things about it; they say positive things. They look forward to us being at places. It's a different story. Amber and I get invited to baby showers by folks in town, the people that are the front-row Baptist sitters. They see me in a good relationship in which I'm a better person. Why should they not accept it?"

Today, Amber Reece and Jenni Harris live in the 150-year-old house in which Will was raised. Amber runs the farm's egg sales and soap making, as well as a new operation that turns otherwise unused animal hides into chew-toys for pets. Amber grew up in North Georgia, in the county just southwest of where I grew up, and her last name shares the odd Reece-with-a-C spelling. She's probably my distant cousin.

If so, I am glad to know a member of my family has found a happy existence in an unlikely place.

SYSTEMS INSIDE SYSTEMS

"In light of the necessity that the farmland and the farm people should thrive while producing, we can see that the single standard of produtivity has failed. Now we must learn to replace that standard by one that is more comprehensive: the standard of nature."

—

Wendell Berry, "Nature as Measure," 1989

As it gets dark one night, Will Harris and I head south toward Blakely for some barbecue.

He tells me this: "If you had told this 60-year-old cowboy that I would have a gay daughter, that I would just be crazy about her partner — and just hoping somebody will say something about her being gay...." He is, after all, a cattleman, and all the best cattlemen have ornery streaks.

"I've been waiting this whole time for somebody to say something about her being gay. I've got 110 employees," he says. "But them cowboys and butchers just love my daughter."

I ask if his politics have changed over the years.

"Good question. I used to be an ultra-conservative hawk, and now they piss me off," he says. "Democrats do, too, but the Republicans piss me off worse. They all piss me off."

On this point, we agree, and speak no more about politics. Will turns his attention to the pastures at roadside. He'd rather point out which flocks of the chickens, geese and ducks we're passing are egg layers and which are "meat birds."

Regardless of politics, American agriculture sits at an interesting juncture. Poll after poll shows growing concern about food safety. A Gallup survey last August showed that 45 percent of Americans actively try to include organic foods in their diets. A majority of people under age 30 — 53 percent — do so, the poll said.

Big Ag has noticed. Just last week, the giant Tyson Foods announced it was "striving to eliminate" by 2017 the use in its chickens of antibiotics that were developed for humans.

But there remains a huge gap between the capacity of a farm like White Oak Pastures, which operates with the cycles of nature, and the huge feedlot systems of the large beef producers. White Oak Pastures can slaughter 35 cows a day. Big Ag can slaughter 100,000.

A visit to White Oak Pastures raises heavy questions about a basic subject: what we eat and how we get it. Can operations such as White Oak Pastures be scaled larger? How can they be replicated by others? And if so, can this style of farming really feed the world? We know American agriculture will respond to consumer concerns. But what will it wind up looking like? Will it look like the de-industrialized operation of White Oak? Or will consumers settle for a slow dialing back, such as the one Tyson's recent action represents?

These are bigger questions than Will Harris can answer, and he knows it. He is already limited by the amount of land under his control. To meet existing demand, local farmers follow Harris' pasturing and feeding protocols on another 1,250 acres of land, producing certified grass-fed beef for slaughter in White Oak's abattoir. But these farmers don't yet find it economically feasible to give up their chemical fertilizers. Which means the only beef White Oak can certify as both grass-fed and organic is the beef raised on its own 1,250 acres.

Harris is also limited by the fact that the organism he's built at White Oak has begun to need resources that aren't in place in Bluffton. One of industrial agriculture's aftereffects was the decline of small businesses in rural towns. Berry wrote more than 25 years ago, "The proprietors of small businesses give up or die and are not replaced. As the farm trade declines, farm equipment franchises are revoked. The remaining farmers must drive longer and longer distances for machines and parts and repairs."

Bluffton's population these days hovers around 100, and it feels like a ghost town, apart from the houses that are occupied and maintained by White Oak employees and a few others, and the old Bluffton Methodist Church. When the congregation dwindled to nothing, White Oak bought the building and began using it for large meetings and to house the offices of a few folks who work in the corporate operations.

"When I was a kid, we could get a baseball game of little boys any time," he says to me one day in Bluffton. "Shit, you couldn't get a baseball game now. You couldn't get a few kids to have a baseball game to save your life."

Harris hopes he can change that. He has applied to the U.S. Department of Agriculture to participate in a low-interest loan program dedicated to providing housing for farm workers. When his application goes through, he says, he'll borrow the money to fill land he already owns all over downtown Bluffton with small houses for the farm workers.

He takes me over to an old building and removes a padlock from its door.

"This was Mr. Herman Bass' store," he says. A sharp local carpenter, Hud Gay, is already hard at work rehabbing the place, shoring up its structure and reclaiming its wide heart-pine floorboards. When it's finished, Harris intends to move the farm-store operation, now part of the same complex of buildings that includes the slaughterhouses, to downtown Bluffton.

A farm is a living, breathing organism, Harris has learned. And nature now demands a few houses and a store if the community is to thrive. Harris says he's content these days with being the "Andy Griffith sheriff" of this community. He rides the pastures, letting his cowboys know if a fence needs mending or if a cow's brisket looks finished enough for slaughter. He rides up to Bluffton and checks in on Hud's progress with Old Man Bass' store.

"This is not a rich man's philanthropic effort," he says. "We got a nice little business and it's profitable, but it's not wildly profitable. I'm not a great fan of money. Money's like blood in your veins. I need enough to pump through my veins. What would I want with an extra gallon of blood? I need enough money to pay my bills. I don't want a certificate of deposit."

After we're full of barbecue, Will drives me back up to the farm store, where I can pick up my car and head off to sleep at an old house on the edge of the farm's pond. Harris had Hud renovate the place, and he added a few new cabins, so now his daughter Jodi runs an increasingly successful agritourism business. You can spend the weekend at White Oak, get a tour of the farm, wake up in the morning and wander out of a grove of trees into a pasture where you might be greeted by 1,000 nanny goats and their kids, whose playful behavior clearly demonstrates why we call human children by the same name.

We're sitting in the parking lot. It's about 10 p.m., and all is quiet. The stars are big and bright, just like in that song about Texas. I ask Will what his friends in the wider cattle industry — folks outside the "the Southern organic crowd" — think about what he's done.

"I still got relationships with the good old boys," he says. "They don't like me much, but they gotta tolerate me. And when I have conversations with them, the first thing they want to throw up is, 'You can't feed the world like that. You know, we have this efficiency thing down, we can feed the world, and you can't feed the world farming like you are.'

"And when they say that, I kinda gotta smile, but my response is always something like, 'Well, I tell you what, I might have that discussion with you, but before we have that discussion, we gotta both stipulate that the Earth has a limited carrying capacity.'

"And they don't want to, but most of the time, almost every time, they'll say, 'OK, all right all right, we'll say that.' I'll say, 'OK, good. Thank you for that stipulation. I will go ahead right now, up front, and concede to you that if the acreage that we have to farm is the limiting factor, you win. You can produce more food per acre of land than I can farming the way you farm. If that's what we're talking about, you win.

"'But if we're talking about the limiting factor for feeding the world being petroleum fuel, I win, because I don't use as much as you do. If we're talking about it being global warming and greenhouse gases, I win. I don't produce as much of that as you do. If we're talking about antibiotic-resistance pathogens, I win. I don't do that like you. I can go on like this for a long, long time, and the only scenario in which, in the long view, your system's better than mine, is efficiency and productivity per acre of land.'"

EPILOGUE

The next afternoon, I stopped by the farm store and loaded up a cooler full of meat and a bag of dry ice for the three-hour drive home. I planned to feed our little two-person family with meat that I knew — because I'd seen the process with my own eyes — had been raised right. It was not one bit different from the country hams and pork chops I grew up on that came from my oldest uncle, Efford, who entered this world in 1898 and thus knew a thing or two about pre-industrial agriculture.

A young man named Louie Schroeder helped me get everything to the car. Schroeder is an Asian-American native of the suburban South. He grew up in Alpharetta, one of Atlanta's more affluent northern suburbs. He went to school at Valdosta State University, where he met John Benoit, who would later marry Jodi Harris. That's how he wound up after college with a job at White Oak, not knowing if he'd stay long. That was three years ago. Such stories are common at White Oak.

Schroeder has risen to run the poultry abattoir. Without Louie and his team, there is no steady supply of pasture-raised, organic chicken. Not to mention the ducks, geese, guineas and the 7,000 heritage-breed turkeys that will have them working 12 hours a day, seven days a week come the holiday season.

I ask him if he likes working here. We wind up talking for about 15 minutes in the South Georgia sunshine, which has the slightest touch of summertime's-a-coming heat.

He tells me he's not sure he'd want to do anything else now, how he's come to love the cycle of a day on the farm, how he's come to welcome a day with plenty of good, hard work to do.

"Man," he tells me as he slams my hatchback shut, "I haven't just made a living here. I've learned how to live."

— Chuck Reece is editor-in-chief of The Bitter Southerner.

First Published July 29, 2014

The Woman Who Ate Atlanta

•••

WENDELL BROCK

The South's most knowledgeable, enlightening and badass restaurant critic has lived in our region for more than four decades. But that hasn't diluted her staunchly Parisian identity. We asked Atlanta writer Wendell Brock to take us inside the world of the deliciously opinionated, French-born food writer.

Her mother left her when she was a baby, and the grandmother who ended up raising her could be mean and difficult. This paternal grand-mere was a terrific cook, though, and a gardener. So when she wasn't bossing her granddaughter or tending to her fruit trees, chickens and rabbits, she fed her sumptuous food.

We should probably mention that this was the Paris of the 1950s, a moment in time when the cuisine was as rich as the culture. At her grandmother's table, the lonely little girl might stuff herself on duck eggs, lamb brains sautéed in black butter, apricot pies and freshly fried beignets. Then, with nothing more than a Paris Metro card tucked in her pocket, she could escape her grandma's smothering presence to wander the City of Light, looking for delicious things to fill her belly.

So while Edith Piaf trilled songs of love and sorrow, and the existentialists contemplated the meaning of being and nothingness, little Christiane Françoise Luc would save her coins to buy a can of pâté de foie gras — or shyly approach the counter of a gourmet deli and ask for a scoop of hearts of palm salad.

SHE'LL ALWAYS HAVE PARIS

When the great Atlanta food writer Christiane Lauterbach describes the Parisian childhood that shaped her palate, there is a fairy-tale, rags-to-riches quality to her story — a touch of Cinderella.

"If you have seen the movie 'The 400 Blows,' it's a little bit of my background," she tells me as she sips a cup of cortado at Little Tart Bakeshop in the Krog Street Market in Atlanta's Inman Park neighborhood on a cool winter morning. She's referring to François Truffaut's New Wave classic, about a troubled young boy who eventually finds freedom by running off to the seashore.

"I had a pretty fierce grandmother, but otherwise, it was pretty loosey-goosey and not wealthy for sure," says Lauterbach, who was born in the 6th Arrondissement of Paris and later moved to suburban Colombes, which she describes as "about as glamorous as living in Queens."

Her mother, a schoolteacher, ran off with another man when she was 2. Her father worked in a factory that made X-ray tubes.

"We were a weird family," she says, punctuating her heavily accented English with girlish giggles, nervous hiccups of laughter and, every once in a while, an unapologetic little snort. "We were definitely a weird family. At the time, it was very unusual. I didn't know anybody whose parents were divorced, who had been abandoned by their mother."

CRACKING THE ARMOR

When The Bitter Southerner asked me to profile the fearlessly opinionated Lauterbach — a longtime restaurant columnist for Atlanta magazine and the publisher of the indispensable, 32-year-old Knife & Fork: The Insider's Guide to Atlanta Restaurants — I immediately agreed.

Over the years, my interactions with Lauterbach had been brief but pleasurable. I met her in the late '90s when I first began to write about food for The Atlanta Journal-Constitution. Later, when I became the paper's theater critic, our paths rarely crossed.

Many will tell you that Lauterbach is intimidating. But from the get-go, I found this short woman with spiky red hair, cat-woman glasses and fishnet hose to be a fabulously fascinating feline.

A bit of a performer, a purring sensualist, a delightfully dishy conversationalist, Lauterbach was sexy in a bookish kind of way: a great person to sit by when you found yourself dateless at the wedding of a mutual friend, a raconteur who responded to tedious questions about her work with dismissive, coquettish jokes.

On the occasion of her 20th anniversary as dining critic of Atlanta magazine, Rebecca Burns, then editor-in-chief of the publication, recalls the scene at which she introduced herself to Lauterbach.

This was 1995. At that time, Burns was a bit of a reticent freelancer, while Lauterbach was the resident diva and exotic. When Burns asked the preening glamor-puss her favorite thing to eat — a question that nearly every critic loathes — Lauterbach responded: "My favorite thing to do when I get home is to get naked, crawl between the sheets of my bed and eat a big bowl of thick, plain yogurt."

In 2010, the Southern Foodways Alliance gave Lauterbach the Craig Claiborne Lifetime Achievement Award. Around that time, John T. Edge, the director of that organization, quoted Lauterbach in the Oxford American as saying: "In my declining years, I'd like to run a dominatrix training school for waiters and waitresses. I'll wear fishnets and carry a whip. I will help them see it my way."

These are the kind of glib comments Lauterbach, who is cagey about revealing her age, tosses off when she doesn't want to give serious answers. They are part of a highly crafted public persona that has been called punk and futurist, difficult and demanding, snobby and unfathomable, quirky and just plain weird.

It's the armor a vulnerable, intensely private woman puts on to protect herself from the prying interlopers who dare to put her in a box. What I was eager to discover, and what I pursued over the course of a half dozen meetings and meals with her, was the complex personality within.

I wanted to see what was behind the mask.

A POLYGLOT GRANDMA

Here are some things you should know about Lauterbach, who has been eating her way around Atlanta since moving to the city in 1974:

- She forms opinions quickly and sticks to them, even when the consequences are costly.
- She likes to eat alone, often sitting at the bar of a restaurant. That way she can gather her thoughts and concentrate without interruption. Naturally, it doesn't always work out that way. Sometimes she needs company so she can try as much food as possible in a single sitting. In that case she prefers men with large appetites. She lets them take home the leftovers, so that she's not tempted to indulge.
- She has an ego. "Sometimes I want to tell people: 'Don't tell me what you think because you are just a prop. You are there so I don't look like an idiot ordering five meals. But your opinion" — she pauses for a second, and makes the sound of a whining cat — "it really doesn't matter."
- She wears Prada glasses. She hates cats.
- English is her third language, after French and German. She also speaks Spanish and gets by in Italian

and Dutch. She has studied ancient Greek and Latin, Russian and Arabic.

- She is fastidious about cleanliness. Servers whom she sees playing with their hair or otherwise touching their bodies are unacceptable to her.

- She has been terrorized by restaurant owners. "One time I moved out of my house, because I got death threats and they sounded pretty serious. .... I reported it to the police, and I moved out for a few days because I was freaked out about that. It hasn't happened in a while, but people used to scream at me and carry on. 'Oh, how could you say my chandeliers are vulgar?' Because they are."

- Once, after a particularly withering review of an Atlanta establishment that shall go unnamed, she was told never to return to any of the restaurant group's locations. She defied the ban, appearing at the company's next new place with two well-known restaurant reviewers. No one got thrown out. She told me that she didn't care what the restaurant owners thought of her: She refused to be intimidated. "I know I am a fat French fuck," she says.

- At this point in her career, she is frequently recognized. Not by her appearance. But by her voice. I have witnessed this.

- She does not own a TV but she does stream video via the Internet. She loves "The Wire" and the Korean TV series "Boys Over Flowers." She's up to date on Netflix's "Unbreakable Kimmy Schmidt."

- She is a Pisces. She likes to knit.

- She is not interested in social media. No Facebook, no

Twitter, no Instagram. "If I had wanted to take pictures of cheeseburgers, I would have made a different career. I'm not super visual." For the record: For a short time during the rise of the Atlanta food-truck scene, she kept a blog, Atlanta Food Carts. The last post is dated Sept. 10, 2010. Knife & Fork has no online presence — and never has in its 32 years of existence. "I don't follow anybody, and I don't want anybody to follow me," she says. "I don't want to be followed!"

- She prefers not to drive on interstates. She is likely to find more surprising places to eat on the backroads. Also thrift stores, which she adores.

- She has two grown daughters and three grandchildren. She is a doting grandma who uses Skype to communicate with her 2-year-old grandson in Washington state. In her home, there is a tiny menagerie of miniature animals that she plays with during these conversations. Apparently, the kid has picked up grandma's favorite word: "Bleh!"

- She has survived things that would send other souls clamoring for psychotherapy, yet I have never seen her play the victim. For example: Her second husband abandoned her with two small children. Simply didn't show for an Easter brunch, where they were waiting. As a result, Lauterbach and her two daughters don't care much for Easter. I learn this when I take her with me to research a piece for the AJC on the Blue Willow Inn, an iconic Southern restaurant in Social Circle, Ga. We happen to stop by the Blue Willow gift shop, which is laden with toy bunnies, eggs and candy, and she opens up about her divorce. By all accounts, she was devastated when her husband left her. "I was crazy about Jeffrey," she tells me. "He may have been a monster. But he was my monster."

- Since starting Knife & Fork in 1983, she has chronicled the ethnic cuisines of Atlanta, from Buford Highway to the Korean boroughs of Duluth. In this way, she can indulge her curiosity for new discoveries, just as she did as a little girl, wandering the streets of Paris. "The thing is," she tells me, "very few people go to a restaurant they have never heard of. Me, I'll be driving around and I'll just be going in and out, in and out, and I make up my own mind. If you don't go to the bad places, you shouldn't be able to talk about the good places, because you don't really know the gap, the difference. So that's very much the way I conduct my life."

This endless pursuit of the city's changing dining demographic is part of her remarkable legacy and one of the reasons she is Atlanta's most essential omnivore.

LOVE & CONSEQUENCES

How did Christiane Lauterbach evolve into the person she is today?

As a young woman, Lauterbach says she wanted to become a librarian. But her grandmother told her she'd never get married if did. She later considered archaeology. "Then I thought: No. Creepy. Bleh! Digging in real places!"

This is how Lauterbach talks, how she entertains me during our first interview at Little Tart. She ended up being a preschool teacher in the Paris public school system. This was partly for mercenary reasons. She wanted to be independent, and by attending teacher's college, she could draw a small salary. So she left home at 17.

"I was very impatient as a teacher," she says.

"You terrorized the children?" I ask her teasingly.

"A little bit. I'm a disciplinarian in many ways," she answers. "So being a teacher, it satisfied my desire to perform. But I was way too impatient. Forty kids in a small Paris (classroom). Bah! Insane!"

In her early 20s, Lauterbach met Volker Süssmann, a man almost eight years her senior, the son of Gen. Wilhelm Süssmann, a German air force officer who was killed in the Battle of Crete. They married, lived in Munich and ate well.

"He taught me how to travel in style," Lauterbach wrote in the 2004 issue of Atlanta magazine celebrating her 20th year as the publication's restaurant critic.

Süssmann was a corporate lawyer for a subsidiary of an American pharmaceutical corporation, and the two moved to New York in the early '70s. She was excited and invigorated to be back in a big city, but soon her world changed again.

Süssmann introduced her to a paralegal named Jeffrey Lauterbach. "I fell in love with Jeffrey, who was five years younger than me," she tells me later in an email.

When I asked her if she was not in love with Süssmann, she replied, "I was a confused and ambitious chick on the make, more than anything else. ... I was also seduced by the New York lifestyle — so free, so exciting."

To stay with Süssmann would have meant returning to Germany. Instead, she and Lauterbach married and moved to Atlanta in 1974 so he could study law at Emory University.

As a European who didn't drive, Lauterbach was shocked by Atlanta, which was then a rather provincial black-and-white town.

"I loved the city and the trees kind of thing," she says in her curious English. "But it was not enough city for me. I was not able to do what I normally do, which was walk constantly — explore. It was very difficult just to even conceive of that in Atlanta, but I was charmed by the vegetation and a new culture. I mean for me, invading a new culture is incredibly interesting."

Forty years later, she is still investigating this strange city, where she has maintained the tricky duality of being both an outsider and an insider.

That is the great contradiction that is Christiane Lauterbach. But is it a gift, or a limitation?

THE FAMOUS THREE-HOLED PUNCH

When somebody gave Jeffrey Lauterbach an Atlanta guidebook, his wife picked it up and thought: "Gee, I could do that." After all, she had always been an adventurous eater. "For me, comparing food experiences has always been part of what I have done — subconsciously."

Soon they were reviewing restaurants as a couple, and in February 1983, they formed *Knife & Fork* with three friends: Bill Cutler, now deceased, and Sue and Steve Kreitzman, with whom Lauterbach has since lost touch.

The Lauterbachs' daughter, Hillary Lauterbach Brown, can't remember a time when the family wasn't reviewing restaurants.

"I remember them doing the paste-up for the layout on the floor or the kitchen table every week," says Brown, who has been proofreading the newsletter since she was a kid and has been the designer since she was a high-school teenager at The Paideia School, a private academy in Atlanta.

According to Lauterbach, the original group met to assign reviews. The couples often paired up to write; at the end, everybody got together again for a group edit.

From the get-go, *Knife & Fork* had a slightly stilted, rather dandified Old World tone that Lauterbach attributes to Cutler. "We used the 'royal we' from *The New Yorker*, which we all read," she says.

Visually, *Knife & Fork* hasn't changed much in its three decades; it has retained its eight-page, three-hole-punched format so that it can be filed in a folder.

"Every once in a while, a subscriber will call me and say: 'I have 25 years of *Knife & Fork*. My wife wants to throw it away. Can I give it back to you?'" says Lauterbach, doing a very good imitation of a creaky-voiced elderly person.

"That's exactly what we wanted, what I wanted," Lauterbach says. "So it's just like a blog, but better digested than most blogs."

One by one, the original writers died or left town. The Lauterbachs divorced in 1989. Since then, Lauterbach has maintained the ship solo, writing in a tone that is consistent with the earliest issues.

Today *Knife & Fork* remains the single most comprehensive record of Atlanta dining history — an encyclopedic, 30-year database that exists in written form and in the brain trust that is Lauterbach.

"She is the holder of our collective culinary knowledge in Atlanta," says Bill Addison, who replaced her as Atlanta magazine's chief dining critic in 2009. "At a time when criticism is transitioning in Atlanta, she is more vital than ever, and her voice remains not just authoritative but enlightening."

John Kessler, the AJC dining critic who befriended Lauterbach after he moved to Atlanta from Denver in 1997, agrees.

"*Knife & Fork* is such a living document of where Atlanta was, the way nothing else has really been," he says. "It's not prettied up and presented at all. It's not marketed. It is a snapshot of a month in the life of Atlanta's restaurant scene."

According to Lauterbach, *Knife & Fork* has 1,500 subscribers. They pay $28 per year or $46 for two years.

"We virtually never go out to eat without consulting Knife & Fork and make a practice of giving it to new colleagues when they arrive in Atlanta," Bill Amis, a subscriber since the beginning, told me in an email. "We currently give Knife & Fork to 11 friends."

And yet Lauterbach is so fiercely competitive that she has been known to ignore subscription requests from some Atlanta food writers and news outlets. Some get around that by subscribing anonymously.

"She does not make it easy to subscribe to *Knife & Fork*," says Brown, who has followed in her mother's footsteps and reviews restaurants for the Athens publication Flagpole. "It's like a speakeasy. You have to know the number."

Apparently that strategy is working. Even in the digital age, when news updates are just a click away, *Knife & Fork* consistently scoops competing publications like the *AJC* and Atlanta magazine.

Brown told me that her father, now a Philadelphia-based financial planner, still subscribes.

"THIS IS INEDIBLE, TAKE IT AWAY"

Lauterbach may not have the name recognition of Kessler or the national readership of Addison, who left Atlanta magazine last year and is now is the national dining critic for Eater.

But in the circle of American dining critics, she cuts a formidable figure. Since 1997, she has been a member of the James Beard Foundation's Restaurant and Chef Awards Committee.

Back in the '80s, when Atlanta magazine hired Lauterbach to review restaurants, the trend in Atlanta fine dining was "continental." Her European background was an obvious plus. In her early days at the magazine, she shared a byline with her then-husband, Jeffrey Lauterbach.

"For Atlanta magazine, we were fascinated with her European savoir faire at the beginning," Addison says, "while she herself found a devotion to Buford Highway, and the cuisines that were much more far-flung. I feel like over the years she has tried to blend the two in the publications that she's written for."

Now, he says, "the rest of the population has caught up with Christiane's curiosity."

Lauterbach has never been shy about talking to restaurateurs — unlike reviewers for American newspapers, who generally try to dine out anonymously.

"I think there is no conflict in that in her mind," Kessler says. "And there isn't in her copy."

Says Lauterbach: "Anonymity is very overrated. ... I'm sure I know the 20 most important food critics in the nation, and they are not very anonymous, believe me." According to Lauterbach and every restaurant critic I know, there is only so much a chef can do to alter a restaurant experience once a reviewer has been spotted in the place.

Lauterbach never makes a reservation in her own name, and she always pays her own way. If she doesn't like a dish, she will ask that it be removed from the bill.

"I have been with her," Kessler says, "when the waitress, the sweet little hi-my-name-is-Kimberly, comes over and says: 'Is it fantastic?' And she goes, 'No, I wouldn't say it's fantastic. This is inedible.' And you'll just see this girl going, 'I'm sorry???'

"'This is inedible. I can't eat it. I don't want it sitting here. And you have to take it away.' And [the server] goes: 'Oh, my goodness! I'm so sorry! Everyone else loves that dish.' And then she'll go: 'I don't care what everyone else says. I hate it. It's inedible. Take it away.'"

In her words: "If you are a restaurateur and I say something bad about you, you should seriously consider that it was bad. And fix it. I am giving you the benefit of my opinion. You could be paying dearly a consultant to find out why this or that aspect of your business sucks."

If that sounds harsh, Lauterbach can be insanely funny, too.

Kessler quotes her as saying the best advice she could give him was this:

"If they bring the wrong dish to your table, if it was meant for the neighboring table, take a bite quick so you can try it."

For free.

CHEF: THAT DISH IS "IMMORAL"

While I was researching this article, Lauterbach invited me to Watershed on Peachtree, a restaurant she has followed since its founding in 1999 by Emily Saliers, of the rock band Indigo Girls, and restaurateur Ross Jones.

Lauterbach championed the Southern restaurant during its heady early days, when Alabama-born chef Scott Peacock ran the kitchen. A protege of Southern-food doyenne Edna Lewis, Peacock won a James Beard Award while at Watershed. He and Lauterbach became friends. (Once, while driving them back from an event in South Georgia in the middle of the night, he hit a deer with his red Volvo, she told me, remembering the moment with some horror.)

But when Peacock passed the toque to chef Joe Truex and the restaurant moved to Buckhead, Lauterbach lost interest. She panned Truex's cooking and wasn't so crazy about designer Smith Hanes' gray decor, either.

Recently, Zeb Stevenson replaced Truex, who moved to Dubai late last year to operate a pizza joint, and Lauterbach wanted to sample the new executive chef's menu.

I make a reservation under an assumed name. We arrive. We blend in.

But when Lauterbach begins to order, her demeanor changes. She tells the server she wants to try Stevenson's new menu items and that's all she cares about. She grows stern and professorial.

Not long after that, Stevenson arrives at our table to say hello. The server has told him about this rapt woman who is only interested in his food. When he asks if the lady has a French accent and the staffer tells him "yes," it's a giveaway.

Soon, co-owner Jones and her girlfriend, Susan Owens, stop by with a bottle of rosé. The meal is impeccable.

When Stevenson swings by again, Lauterbach tells him the half-pint portion size of his chicken-liver mousse is too large, that it could give somebody a heart attack.

"She said the portion size was 'immoral,'" Stevenson recalls on the day I call him to ask about the experience. "That is a verbatim quote. I laughed my ass off."

But he listened to her advice. Instead of serving it in a chubby jar, "I now make it in a terrine mold and cut a slice for service," Stevenson says. "It's quite a bit more moral."

Knife & Fork may have a small readership, but Lauterbach's words, good and bad, are wildly influential.

"In the community of chefs in this city, a kind word from Christiane is equivalent to bragging rights," Stevenson says. "When I am fortunate enough to have her say something nice about me in *Knife & Fork*, you better bet that I get text messages from other chefs in the city saying, 'Hey, I read that. Nice job.'"

Apparently, getting too close to Lauterbach can be a slippery slope.

"It's live by the sword, die by the sword," she told me. "If you want to know me a little better, be aware that it doesn't buy you a better opinion. On the contrary, I may be harder on you because I know you."

"She pulls no punches," Addison says. "A chef being charming and speaking to her at the table for a few minutes does not sway her judgment. She will say what she feels needs to be said about a restaurant."

During the course of our meal at Watershed, I ask Lauterbach if she considers herself Southern after living in the region for so long. She responds with an unequivocal "Nooooooooooo."

She's a Parisian. First, last, always.

A DANGEROUS ENCOUNTER

Lauterbach lives in a beautiful modern space in Atlanta's Candler Park neighborhood. Except for the office where she keeps her files and papers, it is sparsely furnished, with a calm, minimalist aesthetic that reminds me a bit of the house of Alvar Aalto in Helsinki.

The kitchen has an industrial-size stainless-steel refrigerator and sink, and a movable worktable with a white marble top. Stacks of white china, of the sort you might find at Parisian café, are stacked neatly beside the sink.

A central skylight illuminates a small collection of tall, lush-looking plants. Her dining table originally came from a school, and has the markings to prove it.

A pair of white slippers are on the floor next to her bed — Japanese style — and when I comment on the TV, she reminds me that it is a computer monitor, not a television.

Lauterbach rarely lets strangers into her home. But she takes obvious pride in the clean, well-lighted space and in showing me and a photographer around a garden where she grows tomatoes, lettuces, herbs and other edible things.

Like her grandma, who loved her lilacs, ferns and hydrangeas, she is a devoted gardener. But she only grows edible plants. Once I arrive to find her with a reference book on weeds in her hands: She is trying to find the name of particularly invasive specimen — using the approach of a librarian.

But there is one thing beside the door she will not allow us to photograph, even though she points it out with her usual chattiness.

It's a blood stain.

Last July, while her daughter and grandchild were sleeping in a bedroom, Lauterbach awoke to find an invader prowling through her home. He punched her over the eye, and took her car and her iPad.

She later found the car herself, doing the job of the police.

It was, as her daughter Hillary recalls, a horrific moment. When they went for takeout at Taqueria del Sol in Decatur, Lauterbach was so spooked that she only ordered one fish taco instead of her usual two.

That became the family's little joke.

Even though her face was bruised, she didn't stop eating out.

Nor is she likely to.

EPILOGUE: AN UNDYING QUEST FOR THE DELICIOUS

So this is what I learned about Christiane Lauterbach over the two months I spent following her around: She's been abandoned. She's been demoted. She's been bullied and she's been bludgeoned.

But she is a survivor. And she refuses to stop doing what she loves.

When I ask her if she is tired of reviewing restaurants, she seems to have trouble understanding the concept. Burned out? Au contraire.

This feisty, indefatigable Parisian intellectual with the rapier wit and ravenous curiosity is nowhere near pushing back from the table.

She was born hungry — always ready for her next great bite.

— Wendell Brock is an Atlanta-based writer. "The Woman Who Ate Atlanta" won the 2016 James Beard Foundation journalism award for Best Feature.

First Published September 9, 2014

Killings

•••

BY DANIEL WALLACE

*A New Essay From One of Our Favorite Southern Writers —
Daniel Wallace, Author of "Big Fish" — About an Elemental
and Universal Dilemma*

WELL, I KILLED A CHICKEN.
THAT'S MY NEWS.

I cut its head off with a hatchet, the way people do. This
chicken was the first thing I'd ever set out to kill, that I'd
planned to kill over the course of many months, and the truth
is it was weird, exciting, and sad. I didn't kill it to eat (though
it was eventually eaten, in a soup); I didn't kill it because it
was a troublemaking chicken (though it was a troublemaking

chicken); and I didn't kill it because it deserved to die (whatever that means). I killed it because I'd never killed a chicken before and I wanted to have that experience on my list of things I'd done, sort of like going to Venice, to be able to say, as I'm saying now, I killed a chicken. So after talking about it, engaging a few friends in my pursuit (some of whom had a similar desire), hunting for an appropriate venue and, I hoped, a seasoned killer to accompany me, I did it. And though you, you who's reading this now, you who may be a hunter of some kind, a gun owner, a man or a woman who goes out in the woods early in the morning for the express purpose of finding something to kill — you might find this discourse silly and vain. I killed a chicken! But this news, more than almost anything else I could write, tells you everything you need to know about me. It explains who I am and the kind of life I've lived up until right now: the kind of life that not only can go on for almost 50 years without purposefully shedding the blood of another living creature, even a creature whose existence is predicated on being killed, who is born not only to die but born to be killed and eaten — not only that — but a man who felt there was something exotic in killing it, something magical and foreign that requires the assistance of something like a shaman, a guru, an ax-wielding sage.

It also describes my friends, some of whom understood my ambition, some of whom shared it, but none of whom, not a single one, had a chicken I could kill.

My sister had a turkey she said I could kill. But I could tell — even I who had never killed before — that killing her turkey would be an ordeal. That turkey was huge; it would put up a serious fight. I was scared of her turkey. I didn't tell her I was scared of her turkey. I told her I would kill it if I could find someone who had experience killing turkeys and who could be there with me when I did it and after a week of not trying even a little to find someone to help me kill the turkey I told her I hadn't found anybody so she would have to kill the turkey herself if she wanted it dead, which, in the end, she didn't. I think she was just trying to do whatever she could to help, and was willing to sacrifice her turkey for me. That's love.

Other than her, most of the people I mentioned it to thought I was joking, because no one really figured me for the chicken-killing type. When I told them I was serious they didn't get it. What? Huh? What do you — ? What? Seriously? Why would you want to kill a chicken? Why would you want to kill anything?

Most often what I said was, I like chicken. I told them I eat it once or twice a week, which means over the course of my adult life I've eaten parts of thousands of chickens, chickens that were killed by someone else for me to eat, chickens that were once alive, who then were dead, and then — after all the posthumous stuff a chicken has to go through — found its way to my supermarket, my frying pan, my plate, my mouth.

So what I said was: I need to be able to kill what I eat. If someone else can do it, why not me? I need to be able to know what it's like to take a life because I've been dining on those lives forever. If I couldn't do it, I shouldn't eat them, and if I did do it maybe I'd decide it wasn't worth it anymore, worth the killing, just so I can have a nice meal. I said to these people, I've never killed anything before — but in saying that, I realized, that's not true.

I've been killing things all my life.

KILLINGS: THE EARLY YEARS

To the best of my memory, the first thing I killed on purpose is something we in Alabama called a Chinese Grasshopper. My friend Wade and I found a bunch of them at the edge of shade cast by the sour apple tree in my backyard, where we spent a lot of time in the summer.

Kids killing grasshoppers: no news here. But how we killed them, that was, as I would have said at the time, the cool part. With a length of sewing thread Wade tied a small Black Cat firecracker to the grasshopper's back. I'd light it. Then Wade would set the poor grasshopper free. One hop, two, three… bang! Smithereens. Wade and I probably killed close to a hundred that summer.

At roughly this same time, I discovered the magical properties of a handheld magnifying glass. It wasn't about killing in the beginning; in the beginning it was all about fire. The sun's rays could be corralled as they passed through the magnifying glass into a stream of heat, like a laser. Old brown leaves glowed red and orange, smoking as the photons did their work. Then I discovered ants. Ants became ash in a moment. Little black cinders. One moment busily scurrying around, going left, right, back, forward — and then dead, incinerated by the malevolent god who was me. An ant's life is so fragile and evanescent that death must follow it wherever it goes, which would explain why an ant is always on the move. How easily their future is dismissed by a single swipe, a thoughtless flick or fire. Later I would date a woman who wouldn't kill the ants that found a way into her kitchen and marched in a wobbly trail across her window sill. She'd wet a paper towel and gently scoop them up in it, then take the paper towel outside into her backyard and set it down in the grass somewhere, where the ants were free to go.

Plus which, on the insect front: Just the other day I poured tiki-torch fuel down a bee hole in the garden. We were about to have a party and I didn't want the guests being stung.

KILLINGS: A BOY BECOMES A MAN

There were squirrels. There were birds.

Over the years my cats brought home many birds, ravaged but alive, always alive. Cardinals, wrens, rufous-sided towhees, I discovered them bloody, with broken wings, hanging on with the tenacity living things demonstrate near the end. I'd scoop the dying birds into a pillow case, put the pillow case in a plastic trash can full of water, and drown them. They'd struggle for a moment, but only for a moment.

Then they'd die.

I'm interested, of course, in other people, and things they killed — so I asked a few. These are a few of the living things they killed, but most, almost all of them, by accident: baby chicks, a buck, cats, more squirrels and raccoons while driving; lizards, a rat (after which the carcass was thrown on a fire-ant mound), hamsters, birds with a gun, a ghost crab, possums, a hawk (again with a car), a classroom mouse, butterflies, copperheads (my wife has killed three), cockroaches, flies, granddaddy longlegs, fish (lots of fish), snails, lightning bugs (in order to detach their lights to make some flashy jewelry), dogs, and another cat, run over by a friend of mine on Sept. 15, 2001. This one wasn't quite dead, though, so she carried it to the first public building she could find. It turned out to be a mosque, with a service going on inside. Women huddled around the edge of the prayer mats, men in the middle. And here was this blond woman, a crying, hysterical blond woman with a bleeding cat. They let her use the phone, and she took the cat to a vet, and had to pay $100 to have it put to sleep.

THE CHICKEN

Now for the chicken. Like love, I found it when I wasn't even looking. I was in Brattleboro, Vt., with my wife at a writer's conference. My wife grew up in Brattleboro. I got to see her old haunts, her house, imagine what it might have been like to be her as she climbed trees, broke things, created fictional characters with a friend (hillbillies not unlike the one she would eventually marry). We went to visit some old friends of hers, Annie and Rob. They have a small farm where they grow vegetables, raise a few sheep and pigs — and, of course, chickens, many, many chickens. They order the chickens from a company which does that sort of thing (news to me) but they only ordered hens because roosters were trouble. Somehow a rooster got mixed up with the hens in the last order and they really wanted to — What's that you say? You have a chicken you're interested in killing? What a coincidence: I'm a man who's interested in killing a chicken!

Thus it was arranged.

Laura and I drove over first thing in the morning. She went for a walk with Annie, while my shaman and I prepared for what was to follow. Rob gave me an old shirt of his to wear; he didn't want the blood to ruin the nice J. Crew I had donned for the occasion. How ridiculous all this seems in retrospect! Didn't I realize that death is messy, that one doesn't wear J. Crew to a killing? I was such a baby then.

Even with ants and Chinese grasshoppers under my belt, this chicken was different: I could feel it in my own blood as we walked to its pen. For one thing, it was bigger than anything I had killed before, and more alive, and it wasn't damaged in any way; it was, in fact, beautiful.

I stepped into its pen and, because it was a rooster, it walked right to me, and I picked it up, one hand on either side of its feathered body: a luminescent, dark copper this chicken was, and entirely agreeable. It didn't struggle a bit as Rob and I made our way to the chopping block, into which a sharpened ax had been driven. The chopping block was a section from a tree, an oak I think.

It wasn't a long walk from the pen to the ax, but long enough, I thought, for the chicken to object. Only when I placed him on the chopping block itself — one side of his body flat against it — did he realize something was amiss. It tried to flap its wings but couldn't because one of them was pressed against the block and the other was beneath my left hand.

In the right hand was the ax.

Rob had shown me where to cut its head off, and it made sense: right in the middle of its neck between the bottom of its skull and the start of its body. But it wasn't a long neck by any means. It was about the length and width of half a Vienna sausage. I had an opening, briefly: For a moment, its head was still. I held the ax in the air above it but hesitated. *What if I missed?* I thought. What if I missed a clean shot at the neck and just injured it, nicked it. What would I do?

Surely if this happened the chicken would go crazy and I'd freak out and let it go. Then I'd have to chase it down to give it another whack, and then have to live with the hard truth that I'd brought a world of pain to an animal who didn't expect it or deserve it. That's one of the big differences between a chicken and a man though: A thought like this can race through a man's mind in a space of time briefer than a second. Fear, guilt, a notion of responsibility — the sensation of successfully killing what I set out to kill — all these emotions can occur nearly simultaneously in a man. I doubt anything remotely like that occurred to the chicken. I don't know what the chicken was thinking, or how a chicken thinks, or whether it thinks at all; I've read that only humans are capable of this trick. But if I were to go through with this I knew I had to be more like the chicken was and stop thinking, stop feeling, and act.

I came down on it with all the force I could muster, which really wasn't very much: Just as I let the ax fall the chicken turned its head to look up at me, and I pulled back, so the ax came down softly, and at an angle, and I thought I missed it almost entirely, because the head was still there. My nightmare was real: I'd only wounded it. It flapped, I held onto to its feet, white-knuckled, and it flapped, flapped in terror, flapped for freedom, flapped because it didn't know what else to do.

But it was, in fact, dead. Its head was hanging on by a mere sliver of chicken skin. I could see how, had I let it, it might have run around for a while, the way they're supposed to do, but Rob didn't want blood all over the place so he asked me to hold it by the feet while it "bled out." I did; it stopped flapping, became truly dead, and I had done what I set out to do.

My glasses were lightly spattered with blood, as was my borrowed shirt (how right he was about that). I have pictures of this, pictures from the killing, the plucking, the gutting and cleaning the insides out, until it looked a lot like a chicken you and I might buy at a grocery store. The only thing I didn't do was eat it, because I had to fly back to Chapel Hill the next day, but Rob and Annie did: They used it as stock for a soup. Turns out it was too scrawny for a main course.

That's it. And I'm afraid that sums it up, for at the end of a life what else is there to say? That's it, it's over, done, finished. It would be the same from the chicken's perspective, if we allowed it one: I lived and then I died. *Killed, actually, by a man who wanted to know what it felt like to kill me. Now he knows.*

But I don't know, really. Even though I did it, I don't know what it meant to me to kill a chicken. I can't describe it, and the only way I know to understand something is to put it into words. I did what I set out to do, but I didn't learn any secrets. Killing a chicken didn't change me. No one has said to me, *You've changed since you killed that chicken.* Nope. I feel like I know what I've known all my life, or ever since I sat on the curb on the sunny cul-de-sac where I spent my childhood and roasted ants with a magnifying glass: There's a very thin line between life and death. Death can happen in a second. In fact it always happens in a second. Everything else, no matter how long and happy or sad the life is that precedes death, is all just preface. In that second, it will be over, you will be finished, whether I'm there to kill you or not.

Good luck, then, to all the dogs and cats, the snakes and roaches, the butterflies and the wandering buck. Good luck to all you chickens. Watch out for us. Not me — I have no plans to kill again. But there are others out there just like me and they want to know how it feels, and there are others still who don't want to know but will. It's a dangerous world. Good luck.

— *Daniel Wallace is author of six novels, including Big Fish (1998), Ray in Reverse (2000), The Watermelon King (2003), Mr. Sebastian and the Negro Magician (2007), The Kings and Queens of Roam (2013), and most recently Extraordinary Adventures (2017). He the J. Ross MacDonald Distinguished Professor of English at the University of North Carolina at Chapel Hill, his alma mater, where he directs the Creative Writing Program.*

First Published September 23, 2014

A Death Among Flannery's Peacocks

•••

OBITUARY BY KAY POWELL

Manley Pointer, who led the ostentation of peacocks at Flannery O'Connor's Andalusia Farm, has left this mortal coil. The brilliant Kay Powell, longtime mistress of the Atlanta Journal-Constitution's obit desk, pays tribute.

AH, THE MAGNIFICENT PEACOCK – SYMBOL OF IMMORTALITY AND RESURRECTION, GUARDIAN OF THE GATES OF PARADISE, SCREECHER AT FLANNERY O'CONNOR'S ANDALUSIA FARM.

Andalusia's peacock Manley Pointer was not immortal and is not resurrected. He died during January's arctic blast. He lies a-mouldering in his grave off Andalusia Farm's nature path.

The Greeks dedicated the peacock to Juno believing its tail of golden circles on a blue background honored the goddess of sky and stars. Early Christians thought the peacock's blood could dispel evil spirits. Mythology embodies its tail feathers as the evil eye. In dreams, the peacock symbolizes new birth, confidence, even arrogance.

Flannery O'Connor "knew that the peacock had been the bird of Hera, the wife of Zeus, but since that time it had probably come down in the world" when centuries later she ordered a bevy — peacock, peahen, three peabiddies — through the Florida Market Bulletin. She tells us this in her 1961 essay "Living with a Peacock," later titled "King of the Birds."

O'Connor's party of peafowl — she stopped counting at 40 — is gone. The tradition of Andalusia Farm's peacocks, arguably literature's most famous bird, was restored in 2009 by a donation from Col. Charles Ennis of Milledgeville. A public poll named the peacock Manley Pointer after a great O'Connor villain, the wooden leg-stealing, faux Bible salesman con artist in "Good Country People." Bruce Gentry, editor of the Flannery O'Connor Review, prefers that the peacock had been named for a more appropriate O'Connor character in "Parker's Back," the tattooed Obadiah Elihue Parker, a hard-drinking, woman-chasing heathen who sort of turns into a peacock at the end of the story and receives salvation in the garden of Eden.

Manley Pointer's heritage is embodied in mythology, religion and dream interpretation. Yet he was a thoroughly modern bird given to twerking during mating season and ending his life celebrated through 21st century social media. Manley Pointer, 6, died Jan. 8, the victim of overnight 18-degree weather despite extra warming measures taken in his aviary. He died in the arms of his caregiver, April Moon Carlson. News of his death drew 8,000 views on social media. A coterie of young mourners met through social media, dressed in black, and attended the sunset funeral at Andalusia Farm.

About 20 mourners proceeded to the gravesite singing "I'll Fly Away" led by Daniel Wilkinson, a choir director and O'Connor graduate student at Georgia College and State University. He noted that day was his very first as a church choir director and already he was officiating at a peacock's funeral.

At the grave, off the nature trail and marked by a cross of cedar branches, GCSU theater professor Amy Pinney read from The Habit of Being, choosing O'Connor's admonition to author Cecil Dawkins, which includes: "You are asking that man return at once to the state God created him in. You are leaving out the terrible radical human pride that causes death." O'Connor's belief in "the terrible radical human pride" is thematic in her writing, and her peacocks are symbolic of pride. She uses the peacock when she wants to make a specific point about a character.

Wilkinson read from "King of the Birds." He selected the passage about an old man who came to Andalusia to buy a calf and had with him five or six white-haired, barefooted children who were stopped dead in their tracks when they saw a peacock.

"Whut is that thang?" one of the boys asked.

"Churren," the old man said, "that's the king of the birds!"

A COLD KIND OF LOVE

Manley Pointer did not disappoint. Frequently photographed by visitors to Andalusia Farm, now a museum four miles north of Milledgeville, his majestic tail feathers proudly arched during mating season or formed an impressive iridescent train when at rest. Tail feathers shed after his last mating season were collected into a huge bouquet. A freshly washed feather was presented to each mourner, and one was laid on his grave. Andalusia Farm executive director Elizabeth Wylie's son Spencer Cheek has collected clay from the farm to create a permanent grave marker.

And how would O'Connor react to Manley's death and funeral and the ensuing outpouring of mourning and adoration?

"She would make a joke about it," said Gentry, a GCSU English professor and Andalusia Farm board member. In her letters, she makes jokes about their problems. "She's kind of more interested in them after they do something silly or get hurt. Her tendency even though she loved her birds was kind of cold, cool and distant as she was writing in a letter about them."

Sharing Manley Pointer's tail feathers with mourners is very much in the Flannery O'Connor tradition. She gave the feathers to the ladies of Milledgeville to decorate their hats and enclosed peacock tail feathers in her correspondence. Most were received with appreciation. Not so by O'Connor's great champion the poet Robert Lowell. After one of his manic spells, O'Connor sent him a five-foot tail feather. Lowell's comment?

"That's all I need, a peacock feather."

ONE MUST WATCH OUT

Manley Pointer shared the aviary at Andalusia Farm with two peahens also named for O'Connor characters. One peahen is Joy/Hulga, named after the "Good Country People" character whose wooden leg is stolen by the Bible salesman Manley Pointer. The other peahen is named Mary Grace after the acne-faced teenager in O'Connor's "Revelation." While waiting in a doctor's office, Mary Grace throws a book at a woman hitting her in the head. Mary Grace rushes across the room, chokes her and says, "Go back to hell where you came from, you old wart hog."

The peafowl live in the aviary to protect them from predators. O'Connor's peafowl had free range at Andalusia. They created crater-sized dusting holes all over the farm, ate its fruits, vegetables, peanuts and flowers. After O'Connor's death in 1969, The Color Purple author Alice Walker, who grew up in Eatonton near Andalusia, visited the farm with her mother, Minnie Lou, and wrote about their pilgrimage.

The peacocks lifted their tails in splendid display and one would not let them move their car until he finished his show. Walker commented that the farm's peacocks were inspiring, even while blocking the car. Minnie Lou responded, "Yes, and they'll eat up every bloom you have if you don't watch out."

ONE RASCAL COULD OUTRUN A BUS

More recent visitors to Andalusia Farm focused on Manley Pointer's beauty. But few people notice the feet of the gawky birds. (That's why GCSU's literary magazine is named The Peacock's Feet.)

"Flannery was aware of the tradition of seeing peacocks as symbolic of pride, you know, of looking at a peacock and seeing it as ridiculous because it had such a high opinion of itself," Gentry said. "It had ugly parts it was trying to cover up. It's such a mix of what Flannery loved of the grotesque and the beautiful."

O'Connor writes of a telephone company lineman who came to the farm, completed repairs and lolled around trying to coax a peacock to fan out his tail. The lineman trailed after the peacock for 15 minutes or so, then got into his truck and started off. The bird shook himself and his tail rose around him.

"He's doing it!" O'Connor screamed at the man. "Hey, wait! He's doing it!"

The man swerved his truck back around and stared with rigid concentration. The peacock's display was perfect. O'Connor writes, "The bird turned slightly to the right and the little planets above him were hung in bronze, then he turned slightly to the left and they were hung in green."

"Well, what do you think of that?" she asked.

"Never saw such long ugly legs," the man said. "I bet that rascal could outrun a bus."

O'Connor identified with the quirkiness in the peacock. She went through her whole life introducing herself as a person who taught a chicken to walk backwards, Gentry said. "She was telling people it's quirky and so am I, and that's how she wanted to be remembered."

— Kay Powell retired as the Obituaries Editor of the Atlanta Journal-Constitution. She is known in journalism circles as the Queen of the Obit.

First Published October 28, 2014

The Oysterman

•••

BY AMY C. EVANS

"I do not weep at the world — I am too busy
sharpening my oyster knife."
~ ZORA NEALE HURSTON ~

Unk Quick can read the floor of the Apalachicola Bay like
a blind man reads braille. But now, with the bay yielding
precious few of the bivalves that always meant prosperity to
his family, Unk is, at age 73, beginning to learn reading of a
different sort.

"God, bless it!"
We've been on the water for two hours. A. L. "Unk"

Quick is leaning over the side of his aluminum boat, scraping the bottom of the Apalachicola Bay with 12-foot tongs, searching for oysters and calling out to the Lord above. He thinks his prayers have just been answered.

After more than half a century working on the water, Unk has an oysterman's intuition. His hands feel the vibrations coming up through the worn wooden handles of his tongs, the steel rakes at the end rattling in just the right way, telling him he's hit a bed of bivalves.

Unk snaps the handles together, lifts everything up out of the water, swings his body around, opens the tongs, and dumps a small pile of mud-covered clumps onto the cull board, where his wife Gloria separates individual oysters from the large clusters Unk pulls from the reef. They are beside themselves with anticipation. This time, though, Unk's intuition turns out to be false hope: nothing but dead shells.

"There's an oyster on this bay every now and then, " Gloria says.

It has been eight years since I first visited Unk and Gloria Quick in Apalachicola, Fla. I met them when I was in the area to document the seafood industry in this part of the panhandle. Hurricane Dennis had just devastated the area, but it had also managed to clean out the bay. Oysters were plentiful. The industry was holding strong.

Those days are long gone.

In the fall of 2005, I made the first of three trips to Apalachicola to conduct interviews with people in the seafood industry on behalf of the Southern Foodways Alliance.

Of all of the fieldwork I did for the SFA — more than 300 interviews in 14 states over 13 years — this project has always had a hold on me. It was the part of the South I knew the least. It was also where I learned the most: how to sew seine nets and to tong for oysters, what it takes to harvest tupelo honey and cultivate soft- shell crabs. I forged some lasting connections there. And it's the place I visited often in my memory to mine for inspiration for my paintings [also, this and this and this].

For the past eight years, I've wondered what would it be like for me to return.

Finally, last October, I bought a plane ticket. I was fueled by curiosity, but I was also embarking on a personal journey of sorts — an effort to connect the dots between where one part of me started and another part of me longed to be. And it was the fulfillment of a promise to the people I'd met in Apalach, as the locals call it: I had sworn to come back. I hadn't even packed my suitcase, and I knew my return trip to Franklin County was somehow timed perfectly — that by finally committing to making this journey, the universe was offering reinforcement. During every step of planning, there were signs.

When searching the Internet for a place to stay, I happened upon a listing for an apartment situated smack on the edge of the Apalachicola Bay and above, according to the owner, a long-shuttered restaurant.

In 2005 that restaurant was Steamer's, and the dock below was where I first met A.L. "Unk" Quick.

TELL THEM CORKY SENT YOU

Fishermen are a tight-lipped bunch.

Wary of government regulators and anyone who might have a hand in compromising their livelihoods, they're generally not very quick to share, well, anything. At least that's what I found on my first trip to Apalachicola. I had a couple of leads and a few contacts, but I was charged with documenting a wide variety of people and professions, so I had to pound the pavement looking for more. As with anything having to do with getting a story from a stranger, when you have the opportunity to visit with one person, you ask them to suggest someone else, which leads you to another story and another and so on. I'd been eager to interview an oysterman, but I hadn't yet gained a foothold in the community.

Then I met Albert "Corky" Richards, an oyster tong maker in Apalachicola. I visited his workshop up on Bluff Road and got a crash course in tong making, mullet fishing and custom cabinetry. Since Corky crafted tongs for practically all of the oysterman in Franklin County, I asked him how I might connect with someone for an interview.

"Go down to the dock at Steamer's. That's where all of the oystermen are coming in this time of year," he said. "Tell them Corky sent you."

There were dozens of oystermen coming in off the bay that day at Steamer's. Some men were hooking their skiffs to trailers, others were bagging their catch and weighing it on the dock. There was lots of activity and, at first, I just took it all in. I also took photographs. I got the name and number of a married couple who lived up the road in Carrabelle. I chatted up a man working the scale. I took more pictures. Then, as the activity slowed and trucks pulled away, I noticed one more oysterman far off in the distance, making his way to the dock. He was a straggler. A loner. I struck up a conversation as he slowed his skiff a good bit from the shore.

A. L. "Unk" Quick spent no less than an hour with me that afternoon, answering my questions, showing me how to use oyster tongs, telling me about the different parts of the bay. He readily agreed to meet me the next day for a formal interview. Soon afterwards, I met his wife Gloria, who shucked Unk's catch at Lynn's Quality Oysters across the bay in Eastpoint. The three of us made a date to meet at the Apalachicola Burger King for milkshakes. Shakes at the BK have been our standing date for all of my subsequent visits.

Unk and Gloria have been my tether to Franklin County since I last visited in 2006. We've kept in touch, trading phone calls and Christmas cards. I talk about them all the time to anyone who will listen. I spoke of Unk when The Bitter Southerner did a profile of the SFA last year. I have a necklace that I had made from the pearls Unk gave me, pearls that Gloria found while shucking his catch. In a 2013 interview, I declared the sharing of milkshakes with Unk and Gloria at the Apalachicola Burger King to be my favorite meal of all time. After all, a memorable meal is more about the company than the food.

The first thing I did when I arrived in Apalach for my recent visit was to meet Unk and Gloria at the Burger King. It was a Saturday night. The parking lot was all but empty. I pulled up next to what I immediately recognized as Unk's truck, stopping to find my headlights beaming directly onto the booth where Unk and Gloria sat waiting for me, just like they were eight years ago. Only this time, there wasn't much talk about oystering. Instead, we talked about kindergarten.

STARTING OVER

You might have heard tell of the political, environmental and ecological failures affecting Franklin County, Fla., and putting in question the fate of the Apalachicola Bay. Over the past handful of years, the bay has taken many punches: the BP oil spill and the company's use of oil dispersants, overharvesting, the legal battle between Florida and Georgia over water rights that has now made its way to the U.S. Supreme Court, and natural predators invading the over-salinized waters as a result. Today, the industry is suffering mightily. The oysters are all but gone. People are out of work. Oystermen are selling their boats. And lifelong oystermen like Unk are forced into trying to eke out a new kind of living.

On land.

That night at the Burger King, when I was reunited with Unk and Gloria, I passed an envelope across the table. In it were pictures of my 5-year-old daughter, whom they have never met. I watched Unk hold one up and stare at it for a minute before asking, "Is she in kindergarten?" To which he quickly added, "I'm in kindergarten."

Unk quit school when he was a teenager. He floated through, mostly, never learning to read or write. And then he floated out, choosing instead to earn a living on the water. Unk hung up his oyster tongs a couple of years ago, when the fate of the bay appeared to be all sewn up. For the past good while, instead of spending his days sitting on a boat, making use of his 50-plus years of experience working on the water, he spends three days a week sitting in a classroom, reviewing flashcards.

In 1993, Congress enacted the Unemployment Compensation Amendments, which require states to establish and utilize a system to work with unemployed residents whose regular work has, for one reason or another, disappeared. This applies to seasonal workers in general and oystermen in particular. The program helps them to secure alternative employment. The State of Florida has something called the Workforce Investment Act Program that carries out relevant initiatives. More specifically, it offers financial assistance to out-of-work oystermen, so they can get additional education and training, all in an effort to make them more desirable as potential hires. For a lot of former oystermen, this means training to become a corrections officer, an in-demand job with a good salary and state benefits. What it means for Unk is this: getting paid to work toward his GED diploma at the age of 73.

Unk may not have much schooling. He may not be able to read a menu at the local oyster bar. But after the day I spent on a boat with Unk and Gloria, looking for oysters that weren't there, I can tell you what he does know: every single inch of the Apalachicola Bay. He recognizes every bump and crevice and soft spot below, feeling its topography like a blind man reads braille. He can tell the bay's salinity by the smell of the air and the color of the water. Unk can look at landmarks along the shore to tell exactly where he is at any given moment. And he can look at a clump of mud and shells and know whether it's going to be a good day or a bad one. These days, pretty much every day is a bad one.

But that day, out on the water with Unk and Gloria, even though we only had two dozen oysters after five hours of hunting, was a very good day. Back on land, we took our half-filled five-gallon bucket of bivalves back to their house in Eastpoint and enjoyed a bona fide feast.

A GIRL WALKS INTO A BAR

The first time I set foot in Apalachicola, I had my first meal at the Wheelhouse Raw Bar.

It was a cold November night, and I sat alone inside, devouring a dozen oysters and some mullet dip. Outside on the dock, facing the river, were two men — two sailors — warming themselves in front of a Chiminea: Mike from Massachusetts and Richard from Michigan. They lived on their sailboats and made ends meet by doing odd jobs in town. Melanie Cooper Covell, owner of the Wheelhouse, let Mike dock his boat in front of the restaurant. They told me stories about the place and gave me a long list of characters to seek out while I was in town.

I figured Mike and Richard would've moved on by the time I made my way back to Apalachicola eight years later. But nope, they were still there.

After the oyster feast at Unk and Gloria's in Eastpoint, I drove back over the bridge to Apalachicola and my temporary home above the old Steamer's. It had been a long day, and I was tired, but something told me to take a turn toward downtown and see what I could find happening on a Tuesday night in this sleepy little fishing town. Bowery Station looked like it was hosting a lively crowd of locals, so I decided to stop in for a well-deserved drink after a long day on the bay. Within five minutes of being there, I noticed a familiar face at the bar: Mike's.

"I still have all of those blues CDs you gave me," he said almost immediately. I ask about Richard, and Mike pointed to a portrait of him on the wall. He was still around and a celebrated character in town. I grilled Mike about all of the other people whom I hoped to find while I was in the area — people I had interviewed all those years ago. He told me that Melanie sold the Wheelhouse. The old Deep Water Marina and Boat Yard was now condos, and its former caretaker, Wes Birdsong, was living over in Eastpoint.

The next day I got an invitation to join Mike at Wes's house for drinks. We gathered in Wes's garage-slash-woodshop where we drank wine, ate steamed shrimp and talked about Apalach. I asked Wes if he kept anything from the Deep Water Marina & Boat Yard before it was torn down. He pointed to a tall stack of wood in the corner: salvaged floorboards.

Of the many people I'd visited with so long ago, I knew that two were already gone. Corky Richards, the tong maker, passed away in 2008. Later that same year, we also lost Genaro "Jiggs" Zingarelli, a 90-year-old WWII veteran who spent his days printing oyster tags, the information labels that appear on each and every bag and box of bivales, and plied his trade in a time capsule of a shop in downtown Apalach. I knew what had happened to Jiggs, but I had no idea what became of his Franklin County Press. That is, until I went back. Sadly, Jiggs' old print shop is now just another gaudy boutique, selling high-dollar trinkets to tourists.

I found out that Fred Millender, a salty one-of-a-kind character who operated Fred's Best Seafood in Eastpoint, passed away just a few months before my return. He had been in the seafood business for more than five decades and passed away last year at the age of 88. I learned about

Fred's passing from one of his nephews. I had stopped in Fisherman's Choice Bait & Tackle in Eastpoint to say hello to owners Charles Pennycuff and his son Rex, whom I last saw in 2006. Charles was catching me up on how the seafood community was getting along, talking about how shrimpers were now using their boats to harvest cannonball jellyfish for the Asian market. All of a sudden, Charles called out to a large man who had just walked into the store.

"Ask him about the jellyfish," Charles said. The man introduced himself as Tony Millender, a shrimper, and I immediately asked if he was kin to Fred. Of course he was. We reminisced about his late uncle, and then he handed me his smartphone to show me pictures of his latest jellyfish haul. Afterwards, Charles took me to lunch down the street at Lynn's Quality Oysters — now Lynn's Oyster Bar & Retail Market — where we shared a few dozen of Franklin County's finest, the rare few that come through her doors. I got to catch up with Lynn, and had a front row seat to the gossip of the day.

This would be the theme of my trip. It happened again and again: finding people right where I left them, as if our conversation had just been interrupted for a brief moment, and I was circling back after taking a phone call or ordering another round of oysters. I found James Hicks and his wife Oddys behind the bar at Papa Joe's. I met Tommy Ward and his son T.J. at their 13 Mile retail market downtown. And on one particularly fortuitous morning, I happened to drive by the long-shuttered Taranto's Seafood to find Anthony Taranto's son Joey working inside, loading up all of the metal to sell for scrap. Anthony, now 83, came down minutes later, shared stories about his family's old seafood house, and then drove me around for the better part of an hour, pointing out landmarks and reminiscing about the days gone by in this tight-knit little fishing village on the Apalachicola Bay.

WELCOME TO PARADISE

Porter's Bar. Cabbage Top. Cat Point. Picaleen.

To the people who make their living on the water, these names are familiar. They are the vernacular references to the oyster bars or low-lying reefs that populate the Apalachicola Bay. On the day I went oystering with Unk and Gloria, I think we anchored over at least three. When Unk wasn't finding oysters at any of them, Gloria finally called out, "Let's go to Paradise." She was talking about another oyster bar, but she could have been talking about something else entirely.

Many natives of this place believe Franklin County to be the Garden of Eden. Not just a facsimile, mind you, but the Garden of Eden. This was made abundantly clear on my first trip to the area, and Unk and Gloria quickly reminded me of it on this last visit — my first night, in fact, when we met for milkshakes at the Burger King.

"Have I shown you the pearl I found in a catfish head?" Unk asked me.

We had been talking about a particular fern that Unk had told me about on another trip, and I was trying to get more details about it. I thought I had remembered the cross-section of the stem had the initials "JC" in it to represent Jesus Christ. But Gloria corrected me.

"No, it has 'IC', which stands for 'I see,' as in 'I see you,' when God found Adam and Eve naked in the Garden of Eden," she said. I immediately declared that we had to get our hands on one of those fronds. Unk pledged to find one for me on one of our outings over the course of my visit.

And then he made mention of the catfish pearl.

Unk took out his wallet, dug deep into the fold, and then placed a small white bead on the table. It looked like a pearl all right, but it was kind of flat and had a spine-like edge on one side. Unk found it while cleaning a hardheaded catfish, also known as a saltwater catfish. Back up behind the fish's eyes, he told me, are these calcified orbs that people have come to symbolize as the lots that were cast for Jesus's robe. Gloria added that, if you leave the fish carcass out to be eaten by ants, when it's cleaned, it will look like Christ on the cross. (Google knows this to be the Legend of the Crucifix Fish.)

I heard more legends and tales on our drive out to Tate's Hell State Forest. Unk and Gloria wanted me to see the dwarf cypress trees, so they drove me about twenty miles inland to find them. They knew right where they were going, of course. It just took us a while to get there. While we were in the car, I heard stories. Lots of stories. Like the one about Mr. Tate and his own personal hell [longer version here] and how Bloomer Creek Bridge got its name (yes, there were bloomers involved).

Walking through the wilderness with Unk and Gloria, I got an impromptu biology class. They commented on just about every plant we saw, every bird that flew overhead and every muffled sound that came from deep within the old-growth pine forest. On one stop, Unk pointed out an artesian well that he vowed to return to and clean up, since the opening had become covered up with leaves and debris. On our drive back to Apalach, Unk yelled out that he saw one of those Garden of Eden ferns down in a ditch. Gloria circled back around and parked on the side of the road. We got out of the car, and Unk jumped down into the ditch to cut a length of fern. He walked it back up for me to see, but the stem was too dry to be able to make out the initials.

About 10 feet away, Gloria spotted something else. "Is that deertongue?" she asked Unk. He bent down and cut off a handful of leaves with his knife and put them up to his nose.

Deertongue smells like vanilla. Native Americans harvested it for its myriad medicinal uses. Throughout most of the twentieth century, it was harvested as a flavor additive for tobacco products. Unk mentioned that he considered harvesting and selling deertongue himself at one point, but then tobacco companies stopped using it altogether, opting for chemical flavor additives instead.

This is but one more in a long list of revelations about this place, and something that Unk and Gloria have known all along: It offers up everything anyone needs, from sustenance and an honest living to natural cures and signs of faith. But, as with most things, this magical Eden in the Florida panhandle is not immune to the changes brought by regenerating natural cycles or the ills of human folly.

Back in the car, Unk refuses, as usual, to put on his seatbelt. "I wish they'd outlaw those things. I hate 'em!"

This is a man who never sits still for long.

I try to imagine him sitting in a school desk. In kindergarten.

WINDS OF CHANGE

Oysters thrive in brackish water.

Fresh water from the Apalachicola River makes its way

down into the bay where it meets salt water from the Gulf of Mexico. It's a delicate balance. If you spend any time in Franklin County, you'll hear stories about the wind-driven bay. Wind coming from the east brings more freshwater into the bay from the river. Wind from the west brings more saltwater from the Gulf. Oystermen read the wind to know when and where to get their catch.

"They took my living when they cleaned this bay," Unk declared more than once during my visit.

While he hasn't oystered in almost two years, Unk has held onto his rig — just in case. He can't quite commit to the idea of never being able make a living on the bay again — that brackish water is in his veins.

On the days when Unk isn't in school, he works as a janitor at the Apalachicola Senior Center, which opened its doors in 2012, right about the time Unk gave up on oystering. Our first night together at the Burger King, I asked Unk if he missed it. He didn't hear my question. I didn't ask again.

I will always treasure my time on the water with Unk and Gloria, sitting in a boat together, eating Nabs and hunting for oysters. I loved listening to their stories, taking in the scenery and over-documenting the entire event.

They, however, felt defeated. Again.

"This should make you want to stay in school and keep at it," Gloria said to Unk as he pointed the boat back toward shore. "At least you're making money by going to school, because you're not going to make it in this bay."

But maybe things will change. I sure hope they will. If I've learned anything about this place, it's that Mother Nature always holds the best hand.

Back home in Texas, reading back through anthropologist Gloria Jahoda's 1967 book, "The Other Florida," I realize that, while everything about this place seems to teeter constantly on the edge of extinction, what we must really do is keep listening — and going back:

"Middle Florida is a mixture of tragedy and loveliness, every moment spent looking at it is filled with unutterable poignancy. The wind of change will blow. Perhaps it will be a whirlwind. Not yet, say voices that are tired or hopeful or fearful or disappointed, all of them together. All, you understand, have managed to make the music you have heard while you have wandered through their forests and fields and rivercourses and swamps. And always, too, they have said simply, 'Welcome.'"

POSTSCRIPT

It's Sunday night, and Gloria and I have driven an hour and a half west of Apalachicola to Panama City to play bingo. We enter a cavernous hall, and Gloria chooses a couple of seats for us at a banquet table near the back. She settles in, unpacks her ink daubers, and lays out a grid of paper bingo cards. A game is in full swing, but I have no idea how to acclimate to what's going on, so I to head to the snack bar for a Diet Coke.

As I make my way across the smoke-filled room, I notice a sign above the cash window: "Welcome to Paradise."

—*Amy C. Evans is an award-winning artist, writer, educator, and documentarian based in Houston. Amy's paintings have appeared in Southern Living, Southern Cultures, and on CNN's Eatocracy and the Oxford American blog. Her writing has also appeared in Saveur, The Local Palate, and Cornbread Nation 5: The Best of Southern Food Writing.*